Shoes
June Swann

The Costume Accessories Series
General Editor: Dr Aileen Ribeiro

B. T. BATSFORD LTD
LONDON

ISBN 0 7134 0942 8

Typeset by Tek-Art Ltd, London SE20
and printed in Great Britain by
Butler & Tanner Ltd,
Frome, Somerset
for the publishers
B. T. Batsford Ltd
4 Fitzhardinge Street
London W1H 0AH

Contents

List of Illustrations

Since a large number of the illustrations are from Northampton Museum, courtesy of the Northampton Museums and Art Gallery, only those which are from other sources have been credited below.

Introduction

If ever in some centuries to come, the little hat, stuffed coat and
long-toed shoe of the modern fine Gentleman should be discovered
in some Museum of Antiquities, they would no doubt give birth
to many learned doubts and speculations.

THE TIMES, 20 September 1799

Each section in this book begins with a brief outline of the historical background which has a significant influence on shoe styles, as it is impossible to study one aspect of history in isolation. Dress and shoes are an expression of the wearer's place in society and of his feelings, whether desire to promote sexual attraction or support a political faction, or summoning up courage for war, or repulsion after it. Children's shoes are not included, as they follow a different pattern, depending on whether the child is treated as a miniature adult, or something to be seen but not heard.

Descriptions of shoes generally take the order of my 'Proposed Scheme for Cataloguing Shoes', published in *Costume* 11, 1977, except where evidence for choice of dates makes another order more logical. This is basically: colour, material, toe, heel, sole, upper and lining.

Finally, my thanks to John Thornton, former Head of the Boot and Shoe Department, Northampton College of Technology, whose help and boundless knowledge have been generously given over more than twenty years, and to all those friends and colleagues who have been sending me information for so long. Without them, this book would have been impossible.

1
1600-1660
Early Stuart

This is a period of great contrasts: the century begins with the closing years of Elizabeth's reign, with Shakespeare and the other great playwrights still active. She was followed by James I in 1603, a reign characterized by extravagant dress which continued into the early years of Charles I (1625-49), epitomized in the paintings of van Dyck. It culminated in the Civil War from 1642, with the Puritans, Cromwell and finally the Commonwealth.

HEELS

There had been hints of changes in shoe styles in the 1590s, the most momentous being the introduction of the heel, which was very quickly made quite high for both men and women (fig. 1). It probably developed from the wedged shoe and sloping Venetian-type chopine (a platform-soled shoe), when it was felt that the shoe needed to be made lighter. The change was not only for reasons of comfort, but invariably with a new monarch there is a different style: what a major change it must have seemed to contemporaries — a male monarch and Scottish as well, who had a far different character to Elizabeth's. So the footwear was substantial, and yet rather pinched and mean (as was James's reputation), with narrow oval toe and arch.

With the introduction of the heel came the innovation of 'straights', shoes made, like socks, for either foot, and no longer left and right (fig. 3), though some heel-less and low-heeled shoes continued rights and lefts into the 1620s. The fact seems to have been accepted with little contemporary comment — *Day's Humour out of Breath* (1608) refers to 'a pair of upright shoes that gentlemen wear . . . now of one foot, now of another', and was probably the result of the problems of making a mirror-image pair of lasts when a high heel had to be allowed for. Certainly heels and straights arrived together. Rights and lefts returned in c.1800 when high heels were abandoned and, with the development of the pantograph in the early nineteenth century, have remained with us.

COLOUR AND MATERIALS

Shoes were mostly in light colours, especially white, for smart wear (fig. 1); boots were chestnut (fig. 5) and dark brown, black, with a little grey (forty-five pairs of grey and black riding boots were bought by Charles I from David Mallow during the year beginning September 1633). Additional colour came from the binding and decorative 'rose' (fig. 1), or a coloured lace for working wear.

The materials used were mostly leather, including lightweight Spanish leather, and a considerable amount made up on the flesh side as buff or suede, in keeping with the men's buff coats. Suede was also worn by women (fig. 7) and there was formerly a very attractive yellow shoe in Hove Museum. Deliberate use was made of the two contrasting finishes (fig. 6), and in the decoration too, with patterns incised through shiny leather to show a matt contrast (fig. 5). There are many references to waxed leather, e.g. James Master's *Expense Book*, 3 April 1647, lists 'a pair of thin waxt shoes 4 shillings, 19 August thin waxt boots 12 shillings 6 pence.' A red sole and heel appear as early as 1614, on the monument of Lady Doddridge, in Exeter Cathedral. It was to become popular for aristocratic and court wear in the 1630s and continued into the eighteenth century. Indoor slippers were of silk (fig. 8a).

TOES

The toes, first rounded, became square by 1610-20, a shape which was to dominate the whole period (fig. 2), thick and sensible for practical wear, particularly during the Civil War, shallow for slippers, especially in the 1650s. There were a few points from the 20s into the 30s, favoured for example by Villiers before his downfall, and rather unexpectedly by the Puritans. The anonymous author of *Crispin Anecdotes*, 1827, writing about c.1612, quotes a writer of that time: 'a fashion we have lately taken up with is to wear our forked shoes almost as long again as our foot' (fig. 8b). The variety reflects the conflict and divisions in society at that time.

◁ *1 'Lady Dorothy Cary', by William Larkin, in oil, c.1614. Shoes of white leather (matching the colour of the dress), with blunt pointed toe and medium heel. The sole extends up the heel breast, and possibly also forms the top piece. Large open sides, narrow latchets tying centre front, covered with large gold rose of two widths of ribbon, the narrower on top, with turquoise green centre (matching stockings) and spangles. The shoe, apart from the elaborate rose, is typical of both male and female wear, though the shoemaker soon learnt that it was more economical to cut a separate top piece for the heel, rather than a continuous sole which had been normal when shoes were heel-less.*

2 'Henry Rich, 1st Earl of Holland' (1590-1649), studio of Daniel Mytens, in oil, c.1632-3. He wears white boots with shiny brown leather tops, partly obscured by lace trim. Square toe, medium heel. Soft wrinkled leg, typical of aristocratic wear in the reign of Charles I. Flat-soled golosh for protection: it would prevent the heel sinking into soft ground. Butterfly spur leather for attaching the spur and protecting the front of the ankle from the stirrup; it also provided scope for decoration.
▽

Henry Rich Earl of Holland.

3 'The Shoemaker', by David Teniers (1610-90), in oil, c.1650. It shows the shoemaker in his workshop sewing a shoe on his knee. He wears brown leather latchet tie shoes, with deep square toe, low heel, closed sides. There is a similar pair with rounder toe, the sole made straights, in front of his right foot. There is also a pair of men's boots with the wide top of the 1640s, one hung up by the straps designed to pull them on; again the sole is straight. The heels are rather higher than the shoes. Note also the woman's white mule slipper with rounded toe and medium heel.
▽

4 'Charles Prince of Wales', school of van Somer, in ▷ oil, c.1618. Charles, aged 18, wears white knee boots with turn-down top. Blunt, pointed toe, low heel, spur and spur leather, soft wrinkled leg. There was a considerable vogue for boots for walking, as well as riding, from the 1590s to the early years of the 17th century.

5 Youth's shoe, c.1605-13. Of reddish brown leather. Squarish toe overhanging rounded sole, 3-lift wedge heel inserted above the continuous sole and complete rand, made straight. Open sides. Narrow latchets to tie over and through a pair of lace holes on the high tongue. Decoration cut into surface of leather. Very narrow arch typical of c.1610.

SHOES

As to the style of shoes, and strangely to us who assume unisex is new, the men's and women's were similar: the Chaplain to the Venetian Ambassador in London commented in January 1618 that ladies attending the masques 'all wear men's shoes (or at least very low slippers)'. The latchet tie with high tongue continued from Elizabeth's reign, but the side seams became shortened, and the vamp and quarters cut away to leave an oval opening, small on the more practical footwear, but huge for high fashion wear (figs. 1 & 5). They were christened by the French 'drawbridge shoes open to the heel' (1617).

The lace ties ranged from a simple ribbon, frequently in a contrasting colour (red was worn by the poor), matching stockings, sash or other accessories, to elaborate roses of ribbon lace, themselves frequently decorated with pearls or drop spangles (fig. 1). James I said 'A yard of sixpenny ribbon served that turn' (c.1619). Lucy Harrington, Countess of Bedford, wore a simple white and red rose, matching her red stockings, with the masque costume of 1606; and particularly from c.1609-15 there were the magnificent court roses, such as Edward Sackville's, in the portrait by Edward Larkin of 1613, probably dressed for the wedding of Elizabeth Stuart, which Janet Arnold suggests (pers. comm.) were made of four braided layers of green silk satin embroidered with gold lace, stitched through at the centre and decorated with spangles. Mr Sackville's inventory of 1617-19 lists assorted pairs of roses — green, gold, black, with or without gold and silver lace. And they were expensive accordingly. Massinger's *City Madam* (1632) has the following comment: 'Men of mean rank wear garters and shoe roses of more than £5 price'. Otherwise, prices for footwear ranged from a pair of riding boots, 1618, at 8 shillings; 'a pair of shoes for the swineherd, 1632, 16 pence'; Charles I's twenty pairs of riding boots, 1634-5, £24. As Ben Johnson said in *The Devil is an Ass*, shoe roses were 'big enough to hide a cloven hoof', or John Webster, in *The Devil's Lawcase*, 1618: 'overblown roses to hide your gouty ankles'.

In addition to the elaborate roses, the shoes themselves were frequently pinked or slashed (razed) (fig. 7), or embroidered with floral patterns (fig. 8a), occasionally, though not often, matching the doublet embroidery, and worn next to stockings with yet another embroidery pattern, the whole effect being one of conspicuous extravagance.

By the 1630s the roses had lost their spangles and were made of woven material rather than lace, usually silk, matching the garter and frequently also

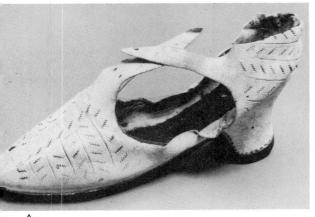

△

7 *Girl's shoe, c.1600. One of a pair of white suede, probably alum-tanned. Round toe overhanging blunt pointed sole of brown leather; 1¼-inch covered heel, sole continued as top piece, made straight. Large open sides. Narrow latchets to tie over and through top pair of holes on high tongue, a style most popular c.1610-30s. Note especially that the quarters are not fully lasted in for about one inch each side of the centre back, a construction feature seen on Queen Elizabeth's buskins (in the Ashmolean Museum) and found on shoes made soon after the introduction of heels in the 1590s, presumably before the development of a satisfactory method of attaching the heel. Top edges tunnel-stitched for reinforcement, the usual method with unlined, unbound leather boots and shoes. Suede sock. Chevron bands of zig-zag perforations between slits incised in the surface of the leather, with braid effect centre front. The lower pair of lace holes on the tongue was for the decorative rose.*

the suit — see the portrait of the five eldest children of Charles I by van Dyck in the Queen's Collection, painted in 1637. With the advent of the war in the 1640s, there were fewer large open sides (fig. 3), and the military shoes were completely closed. There is an ankle shoe with four pairs of lace holes in the oil by David Ryckaert of 'A Shoemaker's Shop', 1630 (Christies, 1976), as well as a long boot and an open-side shoe.

8 *Ladies' mules and shoe, 1640s-50s. (a) One of a pair of ivory satin. Square, slightly overhanging toe; 1⅝-inch covered heel; tan rand. Sole continued up heel breast and as top piece, made straight. Narrow arch. Embroidered with flowers in coloured silks and silver thread. (b) One of a pair of pink and silvery grey silk brocade. Shallow, slightly forked toe of c.1660; 2½-inch dark brown leather covered heel. Straights; wine velvet sock, silver fringe. (c) Of white leather, probably alum-tanned. Shallow square toe, 3-inch covered heel unattached to slap sole. Straights; latchets to tie over and through lace holes on high tongue. Small open sides; originally decorated with rows of narrow braid. The attached slap sole would have been less practical and probably more expensive than the protective overshoe (see fig. 2). All served the same purpose: to prevent the slender heel sinking into the mud and dirt of the streets.*

▽

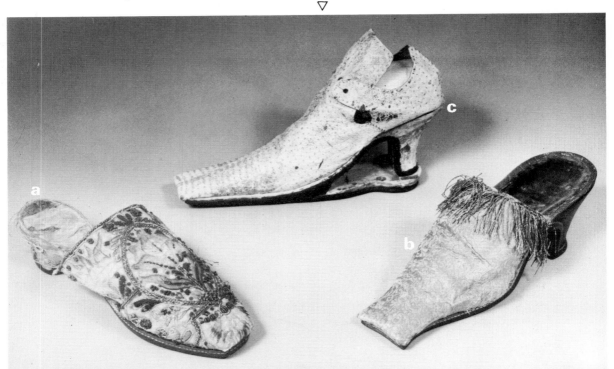

BOOTS

Inevitably, as always in times of war and unrest, boots dominate men's wear (fig. 2), though there is little evidence that women wore them. There had been fashionable thigh boots at the end of Elizabeth's reign, which continued for riding and hunting, turned down at the knee, soft and close-fitting to the leg, wrinkling at the ankles. Occasionally they were worn with great swagger, with one leg up to the thigh, the other turned down at the knee. Charles I as a boy had weak legs, probably due to rickets; his brass-reinforced, orthopaedic-type boots, worn at about the age of eight (c.1608) are in the Museum of London, and although he grew out of the disability, he seems to have been painted in boots more often than shoes. They were becoming fashionable for walking by 1616, and particularly in the 1630s. 'I do not mean that we should be like some of the feather-brained young men at Court who, determined to be in fashion, go about . . . half buried in great boots' (*L'Honneste Homme* by Favet, 1629).

Being supple, the tops could be pulled down and up again, to produce a cup below the knee which became a fashion feature from about 1615. Van Dyck's portrait (1639) of Arthur Goodwin, MP, at Chatsworth, shows him aged forty, wearing cup tops on his light brown boots, wrinkled leg and butterfly spur leather. This became more extravagant early in the reign of Charles I as a wide bucket top (fig. 3). The coachman in Henry Peacham's *Complete Gentleman*, 1636, has 'monstrous wide boots, fringed at the top, with a net fringe', and the same width was worn even during the war: see the Dobson portrait of Sir William Compton as a royalist officer, c.1644 (and see fig. 3) — no wonder they lost. There was a more economical version, with an inverted cup top stitched on (fig. 4). It was especially popular in the 1630s and 40s. All were worn with boot hose (to protect stockings from the waxed leather), which were frequently highly decorative, with fringe or lace (fig. 2).

Under Charles, the spur leather (for attaching the spur) grew into a huge butterfly to protect the soft leather of the front of the ankle from the stirrup (fig. 2). It too could be decorated with pinking and slashing. So the whole effect was flamboyant, arrogant, masculine, according with the militant spirit of the time.

OVERSHOES

To protect the flimsy shoes and boots, there were flat-soled overshoes, with just a toe cap (usually matching) to keep them on, known as goloshes (fig. 2). The flat sole was necessary to prevent the heel from sinking into mud in the days before pavements and tarmac. A few shoes were made with the flat golosh sole attached, called slap shoes, presumably because, not being attached at the heel, the undersole slapped up and down as the foot flexed in walking (fig. 8c).

---

9 Girl or small woman's shoe from Stowmarket, 1640-50s. Of brown leather, pointed toe; 2-inch covered wood heel. Straights; latchets to tie over high tongue. Small open sides, side seams patched. This shoe was found with men's of c.1540-1660 hidden in a chimney of Comb's Ford, Stowmarket, all typical, working class country wear.

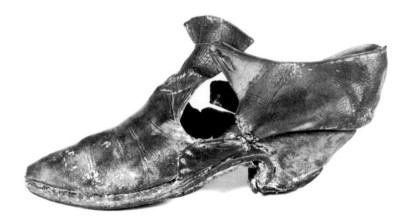

2
1660-1720s

Charles II to George I

That the restoration of King Charles II in 1660 is as much a major event as the beheading of his father eleven years before is perhaps not obvious. But English people signalled their feelings with changes in shoe styles. James II's brief reign had little impact, but a major change occurred with the revolution of 1688 and the advent of William and Mary. The shoe styles as then modified continued under Queen Anne and George I.

The year 1660, with Louis XIV, who made Paris the capital of the civilized world, marks the beginning of French leadership of fashion which was to continue to the last war. In 1665-7 there was a war against Holland, and when one lists the minor wars, such as the Monmouth Rebellion and William III's campaigns in Ireland, it is surprising that it is not until the 1690s that a heavy boot becomes conspicuous wear for men. By then, it had grown rigid, in keeping with the stiffness of other fashions, worn mainly as a riding or military boot (fig. 13). From 1689 to 1713, there were the wars against France and the Spanish Succession, with a break of four years from 1697, until Marlborough defeated the French. Under William the East India Company was formed, the Mediterranean became something of a British lake, and the British spread also to Nova Scotia, Newfoundland and up the St Lawrence river. In architecture it was the era of Wren and Vanbrugh, in literature of Dryden and Bunyan, Defoe and Swift.

Given the power of France and Charles II's French background, it is inevitable that French fashions dominated England. Boots, with their reminder of Civil War and aggression, disappeared as fashion wear, though they were retained for riding.

COLOUR AND MATERIALS

For men, black and browns were the usual colours in the earlier years. *Le Nouveau Galant*, 1678: 'souliers se portent noirs lustrez' — and the illustration shows a buckle shoe with a high tongue. The red sole and heel, a French court fashion, became more common wear in England: see the 1680 oil by Kneller of the giant, Anthony Payne, halberdier of Plymouth Citadel (in Truro Museum), in tan shoes with red soles and heels, small open sides, the silver buckle, with single prong hooked into a buttonhole. Randle Holme, *Academy of Armoury and Blazon*, 1688, mentions India red for sole edges. White leather was worn for court (fig. 10). Some buff or suede leathers continued. Indoor slippers were of brocades (fig. 14a), with leather for working women, and also for women's shoes. The entry for 16 November 1665, in Pepys' *Diary* records 'My Lady Batten, walking through the dirty lane with new spick and span white shoes, she dropped one of her galoshes in the dirt'. But the majority were of brocades, with some velvet (fig. 16), silks and satins, embroidered for full dress, and with extensive use of appliquéd braids, producing a striped effect (fig. 11). Randle Holme's *Academy III*, 1688, mentions 'laced shoes have the upper leathers and edges of the shoe laced in orderly courses with narrow galloon lace of any colour'. By about 1690 there was a broad band of braid up the centre front (plate 1b), and often too at the back of the heel and quarters. The broad vamp braid is shown on a tile in Sintra Palace in Portugal, 1670, with alternate plain and brocaded stripes, on a woman's shoe worn for riding. The style may have come with Charles's Portuguese queen. Bullion lace was used to such an extent that its import was prohibited in 1711 (plate 1a). Defoe's *Everybody's Business, Nobody's Business*, 1725, describes a country girl becoming a servant in London: 'Her neat's leathern shoes are now transformed into laced ones with high heels.'

A conspicuous feature of women's shoes was the white kid rand, used in attaching the sole. It is seen as early as the mules of Henrietta Maria (fig. 16) and was to continue to the 1760s. Darker inconspicuous ones had been used previously (fig. 5).

TOES

The long, square toe came with Charles from France (fig. 10), though some had appeared in the 1650s: there is one in the outline of a shoe dated 1659 in the lead from Nether Worton church roof, Oxford-shire. Randle Holme *Academy III*: 'Shoes, according to the fashion of the Toes or Noses are sometimes round, others square, then forked, and others turned up like a hook'. There are references to 'long shoes', e.g. Evelyn's *Tyrannus or the Modes*, 1661. The forked toes are clearly shown in Lely's drawings for 'Knights and Heralds in the Garter Procession',

10 *'Charles II Enthroned', by J.M. Wright, in oil, 1661. In coronation robes, with white leather shoe. Shallow square toe, high red heel. Red sole. Straps* ▽ *fasten over high tongue with a buckle set with red and blue stones. This is one of the earliest portraits showing the new fashion for buckle shoes.*

c.1665, and also his portrait of Henry Howard, 6th Duke of Norfolk, 1677. They are worn also by Anne Churchill, Countess Sunderland (1699-1716) in the Althorp portrait, and in the Kneller portrait of the

row square domed toe, medium-high red leather-covered heel, white stitched. Possibly buff rand. Open side, revealing red stocking. Straps fastening over high tongue with gold buckle set with red stones. The catalogue of the National Portrait Gallery Exhibition of Irish portraits dates this portrait 1697. Either date would be acceptable for the domed toe, though it was much more common in 1697, but open sides had ceased long before then.

11 'Lady Catherine and Lady Charlotte Talbot', by J.M. Wright, in oil, 1679. The teenage girl is in olive-coloured shoes with gold braid appliqué. Nar-

▽

Countess of Mar in riding dress of 1714-15 in the Scottish National Portrait Gallery. There are a number of examples of women in square toes up to the 1680s: Catherine of Braganza is shown on a Map of London, 1682, in striped braided shoes, square toe.

By 1676 some were beginning to be blocked, the end presenting a curved, classical pediment shape (fig. 11); see the 1676 portrait of the 3rd Lord Cornwallis at Audley End. They were quite narrow under William and Mary and Anne, but began to widen in the 1690s. St Jean's 'Homme de Qualité', 1693 and 1694, are fairly wide, with the buckle set to one side. The wide dome is typical of the reign of George I

(figs. 12, 14a & b). In the Kneller portrait of the Duke of Marlborough at Althorp, 1711-12, he wears a black shoe with wide, square domed toe, medium heel, very high tongue with gold buckle. William III's effigy (died 1702, first exhibited 1725), in Westminster Abbey, has the same toe on a white shoe.

Such a toe may have been acceptable for a man of standing, but could scarcely be considered feminine. Perhaps because of the growing dominance of female society, for the first time, women's toe shapes diverged from men's: some continued to wear the shallow toe, but most decided a point was more elegant (or possibly more of a hobble?), and the first points

---

12 'George I in Coronation Robes', studio of Kneller, in oil, c.1714. Shoes of fawn leather with the wide square domed toe typical of his reign. High flared tongue with narrow straps fastening over it, and buckle set with dark red stones.

△

13 One of a pair of men's boots of black leather, c.1705. Square toe, 3-inch high stacked heel, oval in section, wooden pegged; straights. Rigid leg to knee, seamed at centre front, wide top covering lower thigh. Top edge has 2 rows of tunnel stitching. The spur with D-shaped buckle rests on the spur block (modified butterfly spur leather missing). This is the military boot, derived from the early 17th-century styles. Both leg and top are of lighter leather until the rigid leg appears in 1688. It was to continue as a military boot to the 1730s.

14 Men's mule slipper and shoe, 1707-20s. (a) One of a pair of slippers of pink, beige, green etc. bizarre silk of c.1707-8. Wide square domed toe, $2\frac{3}{8}$-inch covered flared heel, wooden pegged. Straights; pink suede rand, white stitched. Yellow silk sock, leather bound; tan leather lining. It originally had 2-inch wide silver braid at vamp top. Typical indoor wear 1700-20s. (b) One of a pair of dark maroon leather shoes. Wide square domed toe, 2¼-inch black leather-covered wooden heel, flaring to a leather top piece pegged on, hollowed in centre for lightness. Black sole edge; straights. High tongue lined with pink silk, intended to turn over in wear to form 'Cupid's bow'. Edges reinforced and decorated with buff tunnel stitching. Shoes without buckle straps are less typical.

▽

15 One of a pair of men's buckle shoes of black leather, 1680s. Rather shallow round, slightly over-hanging toe, 2-inch reddish leather covered heel, wooden pegged. Brown rand; straights. Narrow straps to buckle over high tongue; there is a buttonhole cut near the seam at the start of the straps, where they may have been extended to convert the shoes from tie to buckle fastening; or more likely, the buttonhole could have served for the anchor-type chape, especially as the tunnel stitching continues across the strap seam. Small open sides; V-dip at back seam.

▽

16 Mule slipper worn by Queen Henrietta Maria (d.1669), c.1660-65. One of a pair of red velvet, embroidered with silver. Narrow square overhanging toe, high black leather covered heel, D-shaped top piece. White kid rand; straights. Red velvet sock, silk lining.

▽

began to appear in the late 60s. The portrait of Mme de Montespan has a blunt point developed from a tapered square like Henrietta Maria's (fig. 16). There is a similar, rather deeper toe on the monument of Mary Langton, in Cottesbrooke church, Northamptonshire, 1676. By the 90s the point was made quite deep (Randle Holme's reference to 'hooked'), but is gradually replaced by a needlepoint (plate 1). See the shoes worn at a ball in honour of Queen Anne in 1710 in Bury St Edmund's Museum. The needlepoint toe was to last to the 1760s.

HEELS

The heels of men's and women's shoes at first were similar, i.e. high for both sexes (fig. 10). Steele, in *The Spectator*, 1711: 'I am mounted in high-heeled shoes with a glazed wax-leather instep'. The heels were made of wood and covered with leather to match or contrast with the shoes. There were more stacked heels for men; there is a fine stacked one on a male supporter on the monument to Mary Baynton, St Mark's Church, Bristol, 1667. Most of the riding boots used stacked heels (fig. 13). Randle Holme, *III*, 1688: 'Shoes in the fashion of heels, are some flat and low-heeled, or with wooden high heels, broad and narrow; others leather heels, which some term Polony heels.' Wooden heels dating from the 1690s to 1725 have been excavated at Colonial Williamsburg: high thin, high thick and low thick.

The construction of the covered heels is what is today known as a louis, but the back line is usually straight, rather than a related curve. Up to c.1700 they were quite slender; see the 1661 one at Nether Worton Church. The men's shoes with wide domed toe of George I's reign have a massive heel to balance, flaring out from the seat, hollowed up in the centre for lightness (figs. 14a & b).

SHOES

The latchet tie shoes continued from the first half of the seventeenth century, but the popularity of open sides declined (fig. 10), most of the women's fabric top shoes being closed soon after 1660, though some continued for men into the 80s, possibly because leather shoes were made by the same makers. Randle Holme says (1688): 'Close shoes are such as have no open in the sides of the latchets, but are made close up like an Irish brogue. They are to travel with in foul and snowy weather.' The side seam was cut straight from the 1670s to 1702 (fig. 13), springing from close to the back seam. It is shown on engravings of men and women by Jean de St Jean, 1673-8. The William III effigy, 1702/1725, has a dog-leg side seam.

The ribbon ties, too, changed. There were multiple ribbons in the reign of Charles II: Lely's drawings of 'Knights and Heralds in the Garter Procession' have floppy bows, and there a few butterfly bows. They changed to a much stiffer, formalized wide bow, projecting beyond the shoe from c.1690 to 1710, first shown on the 1676 drawing of the marriage of Charles II to Catherine of Braganza (1662), though his funeral effigy of 1685 in Westminster Abbey fastens with a ribbon, to which is attached a bunch of white and figured ribbons. Shepton Mallet almshouses paid 3 shillings 6 pence in 1699 for a 'strong pair of russet leather shoes with a pair of blue points to tie them.'

But Pepys signals an innovation in his *Diary*, 22 January 1660: 'This day I began to put on buckles to my shoes' (see fig. 10). The buckles were small, oblongs or ovals, set with stones or glass 'paste', though Evelyn in his *Diary* entry for 18 October 1666 indicates that buckles did not become a general fashion immediately: 'The first time H.M. put himself solemnly into the Eastern fashion, changing . . . shoe strings and garters into buckles, of which some were set with precious stones.' Adapted from the latchet tie, the early solution was a buckle with stud to lock through a hole in the latchet (fig. 15). The other strap was then cut longer to fasten the shoe. Both straps tended to be narrow, and the buckle had a single spike, and sometimes appeared on the side of the shoe, rather than the centre front. Some shoes during the reign of Charles II had a similar false strap, rather stiff, slotting through the buckle, more common on women's footwear. From the beginning, buckles were treated as jewellery, transferable from one shoe to another, and could be used through a slot buttonhole on other garments, as required. There is a portrait of Charles II of c.1670 by Verelst and another c.1680, with a buckle, and blue and white ribbons — the best of both worlds.

With the heavier shoes under George I, a larger buckle was more appropriate, and the straps were cut wider to carry it, and of equal length, to take a different chape: two sets of double prongs, one of which anchored the buckle on the strap, while the other acted as fastener. A few buckles with anchor chape requiring a buttonhole continued into the 1730s. As so little of women's shoes was visible, just a toe tip beyond the long skirt, there was little point in wearing an attractive buckle, the prongs of which were liable to catch in petticoat and dress. So women retained the latchet tie style after the majority of men had changed to buckles.

Throughout the period the buckle or lace was set high on the instep, with the tongue extending above (fig. 10). During the reign of Charles II the tongue followed the rather droopy line of the rest of the costume and was allowed to fold over. This was formalized and stiffened with a lining from c.1690 through the 1710s. The tongue was cut into fancy shapes, so that the contrasting lining (red was most popular on men's black shoes) took such forms as the cupid's bow (fig. 14b). Again, this detail would not have been visible in women's shoes in wear, though some had the cupid's bow regardless, and some were vandycked, with zig-zag top line (fig. 17).

OVERSHOES

For protection, there were a few goloshes and slap soles. But so many surviving examples are unworn, one suspects they were primarily of novelty value. The more practical solution adopted by women was clogs and pattens. The clog, which scarcely deserved the name, was a small wooden wedge to fit under the arch of the shoe, covered in strong leather extended under the ball and toe, with a socket at the other end to take the shoe heel. The whole was underlain by a flat sole which effectively prevented the shoe heel from digging into soft ground (plate 1). The most practical version had a leather golosh with latchets to tie over the shoe. But the majority had just a brocade-covered leather latchet, of similar material to the shoe. The Verney Memoirs of 1681 request 'Pray send me one of your shoes to have a pair of clogs fitted to it, that you may walk about without taking in wett at your feet.'

The pattens were the same, with the addition of an iron ring or four-lobed hoop underneath, to raise the wearer even further. The four-lobed type is illustrated by B. de Moncony's entry for 2 June 1663 in his *Voyage d'Angleterre*: 'Cela fait un assez grand bruit sur le pavé'. In 1705 each girl at St Martin-in-the-Fields school was given a pair of pattens 'to keep her feet clean and tite' (sic). Randle Holme noted: 'What a patten is your gentlewoman will tell you; it is a thing of wood like a shoe sole, with straps above it to tie over the shoe, having an iron at the bottom, to raise the wearer thereof from the dirt; by means whereof clean shoes may be preserved though they go in foul streets'. Defoe in 1725 implied that the wooden pattens were country wear to be kicked away for leather clogs in town, and they were obviously something of an impediment. Pepys' *Diary* entry for 24 January 1660 reads: 'Called on my wife and took her to Mrs Pierce's, she in the way being exceedingly troubled with a pair of new pattens and I vexed to go so slow, it being late.'

Netscher's picture of a lacemaker of 1664 shows a wooden-soled shoe with black leather uppers, smart square toes and large open sides, from which the later Lancashire clog may have descended. The London Gazette of 1681 mentions a short pair of clog-boots, though these sound distinctly masculine. The *Warrants* of Queen Mary II, August 1694 to January 1695, show she bought five pairs of satin sabots laced with gold or silver lace, presumably a Dutch influence.

BOOTS

Boots were worn for riding, the cavaliers' wrinkled boot leg began to stiffen and straighten in the 1660s, the whole boot being of stronger leather with a high wax finish. *Voyage to the South Sea*, 1712, says 'leather so dressed that it is not inferior to iron, like our jackboots'. The top no longer flopped down, but was worn a practical thigh length; perhaps the great winter frosts had some effect (fig. 13). The style probably came from Holland, and the 'Reception of the Prince of Orange in 1688' shows him in a rigid-legged boot, and there is a painting of Althorp Park, 1677, by J. Vorstermans with a horseman in straight-legged boots of the Marlborough type. It is the cavalry boot par excellence from the Battle of the Boyne, 1690, through the Marlborough Wars. The toes were a practical width and square, more being made domed under George I, when the war was over, though Hereford Museum has a boot reputedly worn at the Battle of Blenheim, 1704, with a 1¾ inch square domed toe, and top cut away at the back of the knee, for ease in riding.

The softer leg boots were mainly continental, using suede leather, front lace, or side buttoning. The engraving 'Le Mercure Galant' of a milliner's shop, 1678, illustrates the King's riding boots with a row of gold buttons at the centre front. There is also a pair of fawn leather side button boots in the Museum of London, with the narrowish square domed toe of the 1690s. They date mainly from the last quarter of the seventeenth century, but Rugge's *Diurnal* for 11 October 1666 states: 'In this month H.M. and the whole Court changed the fashion of their clothes . . . buskins, some of cloth, some of leather, but of the same colour as the vest ornament.' Women continued to wear boots for riding, and Pepys' *Diary*, June 1666: 'Walking in the Galleries at White Hall I found the Ladies of Honour dressed in their riding garb with boots and doublets, just for all the world like mine.' And at the end the century Swift recommends Stella in a letter to buy a pair of good strong boots.

It may have been the softer boots, or rather the poor state of the roads and increased travel which produced the protective gambado: a rigid casing, hopefully waterproof, worn on horseback over riding

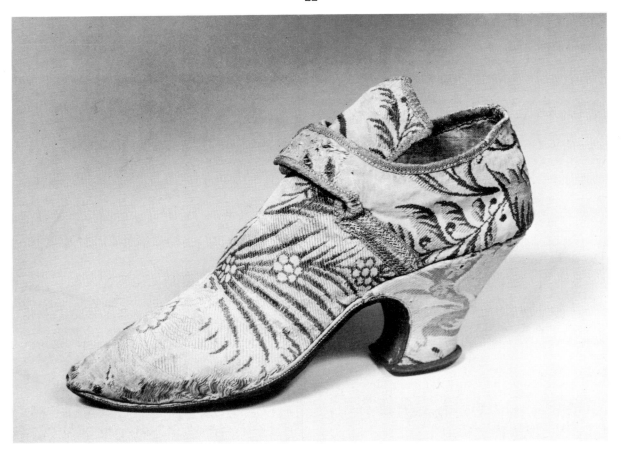

17   One of a pair of lady's green and pink silk brocade buckle shoes, c.1700-10. Pointed upcurved toe, 2½-inch covered louis heel. White kid rand; straights. Narrow straps to buckle over high, slightly peaked tongue lined with green silk, which may have turned over in wear.

---

boots. In 1661 F. Hawkins, *Youth's Behaviour*: 'Gambado — large leather cases or stirrups to keep the legs clean in riding.' The amount of leather in the jack boot inevitably meant a very expensive boot. In 1673 the Duke of Hamilton paid £2 14 shillings for shoes, £12 for boots. So gaiters or spatterdashes were used for cheapness over shoes, most being of leather, with some suede, and fastening up the side with interlocking loops drawn through 'buttonholes'.

SLIPPERS

Indoor slippers were in mule form, though by 1678 the word 'mule' was used only for the sixteenth century style chopines with platform sole. Randle Holme uses 'slipper' or 'pantable': 'Slippers are shoes without heel quarters.' There was a variety of colours and materials, worn by both sexes (figs. 14a, 16). They continued to appear as decorative and symbolic features in Dutch paintings. Jan Steen's 'Morning Toilet' of 1663 shows a bedroom with women's mules on the floor, having red soles, and he illustrates a similar pair for men in the next year. They were worn in winter as well as summer. There is a very fine pair with the toilet set bought in France c.1728 by the 4th Earl Dysart in Ham House, of blue and silver brocade, with square domed toe, rather narrow, medium high, red leather-covered heel, and tan continental rand.

3
1720s-1790

George II and George III to the French Revolution

18 'Marriage à la Mode, Shortly after the Marriage', by William Hogarth, in oil, 1743. The lady wears light soled, silk brocade buckle shoes, toning with her dress; needlepoint toe, medium heel. The men's are all black leather and buckled. The steward, a middle-aged man, is in shallow square toes, no longer fashionable, and low heels; a practical, comfortable shoe. The young lord wears more pointed toes, though not as sharp as his lady's, and high red heels.

George II came to the throne in 1727, George III in 1760. The Whigs were in power from 1714 until 1761, succeeded by the Tories, with a brief break in 1782. There were wars with Spain in 1739, the rising in Scotland of 1745, followed by the War of the Austrian Succession in 1748-56. It was quickly followed by the Seven Years' War, trouble in Canada and India, which was beginning to exert greater influence on life in England, and finally the American War of Independence in 1775, resulting in the loss of the colony.

19 L'Art du Cordonnier, by F.A.P. de Garsault, published Paris, 1767. Man's buckle shoe with quite low stacked heel, wooden pegged (f) and fig. AA, the unfinished sole, made straight with pointed toe. Fig. 3 man's sabot. Fig. 4 man's overshoe with low quarters. Fig. 2 man's mule slipper with low covered heel. Fig. 5 sole of foot. The accompanying text suggests the walker should wear a straight shoe on alternate feet on alternate days, to keep the shape. Fig. 6 sole of a left shoe worn by a hunter who had shaped shoes made from lasts moulded on the shape of his feet: the earliest 18th century examples of rights and lefts known. D, C, and E heels for women's shoes. F and G vamp and quarters for women's shoes. L, M and N women's shoes in the making. O woman's finished shoe with wedged heel, straps for buckle, the one visible has buttonhole for anchor type chape, and straight side seams, bringing buckle low on instep. P women's clog overshoe. R and Q men's and women's legs showing the shoes in wear.

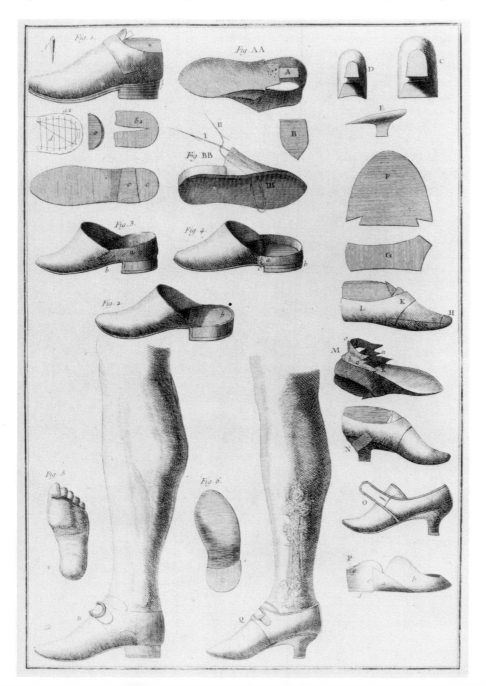

20 'The Rev. Carter Thelwall and Family', by
George Stubbs, in oil, 1776. Set in the countryside,
he is dressed for riding, in close-fitting top boots in
strong, but supple leather, the legs wrinkled in wear.
Oval toe, low heel. Brown turndown top, with
anchoring strap above the knee.

The period closes with the upheaval of the French
Revolution in 1789.

The great country houses were modernized, Baroque changing to Rococo and Adam styles, civiliza-
tion and culture spreading out into the countryside.
In town there were the first effective acts for paving:
London in 1762, county towns such as Northampton
in 1778, which were to permit less practical heels for
women. Boot scrapers by the door came into use
after 1760, and they indicate that the gentry could
by then walk about instead of going everywhere in
carriage or chair. Bath began to rival London as a
centre for fashionable society, the first Master of
Ceremonies, Beau Nash, who succeeded in banishing
boots and swords from drawing rooms, dying in 1762.
In total contrast, the Industrial Revolution began
about the middle of the century. It barely touched
the shoe industry, though the roads which were
necessary for all these developments facilitated their
transport all over the country.

For this period it is easier to consider the two sexes
separately, since their shoes took distinct styles.

MEN'S

With the wars, the growing empire, and the beginnings of the Industrial Revolution, men's shoes
suddenly became staid, in practical dark colours, the
only flamboyance being the buckles.

There were japanners of shoes from 1725 and
japanned pumps mentioned in 1750, though this
probably referred to a high polish, rather than patent
leather, which was not used for footwear until after
1790.

COLOUR AND MATERIALS

Men's shoes were of black or dark brown leather,
with occasional red heels for court and smart wear,
and red sole edges up to c.1760. There was a little
velvet for dress wear and satin for dancing. The
leathers became lighter in the 80s, presaging change,
with lighter colours too, such as white, red, yellow.
The riding boots remained dark, with the addition
from the 1730s of a light 'top' on the top boots
(fig. 20).

TOES

The men's square domed toe died out at the end of
the 20s, though the cornonation portrait of George II
by Charles Jervas, 1727, shows him in a narrow domed

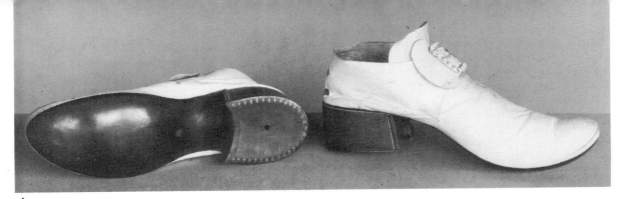

21 Shoes from the effigy of the 2nd Duke of Buckingham, carried at his funeral, January 1736, aged 19. Buckle shoes of white alum-tanned leather. Oval toe, sharply-upcurved, with puff, overhanging and pleated onto domed brown sole, unworn; 1¾-inch red leather covered, slightly flared heel, wooden pegged. No rand, which suggests turnshoes made especially for the effigy. Very long staggered side seam. Silver buckles set with pastes, pitchfork-type chape.

22 Man's jack boot, mid-18th century. Of strong black leather. Square overhanging toe, 2½-inch stacked leather heel, wooden pegged. Straights. Rigid knee-high leg, front seamed, with softer flap to thigh. Leather straps inside to pull on. Spur leather with spur of c.1630, which does not fit on the spur block at the back. The spur leather and thigh flap have matching decorative stitching, which also served to reinforce the leather (i.e. an old spur has been re-used). There is similar shield-shaped decorative stitching on the sole, indicating the boot was made purely for riding. From Burderop Park, Wilts. There are comparable boots (without the decoration) in both Diderot's Encyclopédie and Garsault's L'Art du Cordonnier.

toe. It was replaced by a point, which continued to the end of the century with some variation. At first they were sharply pointed and turned up like a hook (fig. 21). In 1734 the London Magazine mentioned 'a fop in Spanish leather pumps without heels and burnished peaked toes.' But after 1740 the majority were blunter, more comfortable, until they became sharper again in the 70s. In 1768 for the Dragoon Guards the boots were to be round toed. There is a pair of knee-high boots in the Victoria and Albert Museum of this date with a blunt pointed toe.

There are mentions of square toes. Today we tend to refer to the older generation as 'square'; in the eighteenth century it was 'square toes'. In Smollett's Humphrey Clinker, 1771, Matthew's nephew frequently refers to him as 'old square toes', and there is a 1784 Rowlandson caricature, 'A College Scene' of a son scrounging money from his father, using the same term. It is interesting to see how long the memory of style lived on, for there are no depictions of them after the 1740s (fig. 18).

HEELS

Men's heels dropped to one inch, the usual modern height (though many were still covered, rather than stacked leather). Swift's Voyage to Lilliput, 1726, may be based on a more recent memory, where there are two parties, the Tramecksan who wear high heels and represent the Tories, high church party, and the Slamecksan who wear low heels, for the Whigs, or low church party favoured by George I. George II is said to have 'favoured' both; hence the hobble. There was a brief resurgence of high heels worn by a very limited number, in the 40s to 50s (fig. 18). Of Smollett's Ferdinand Count Fathom, in 1753, he makes the following comment: 'the heels of his shoes were so high as to raise his feet three inches at least.' There is

△
23 Man's buckle shoe, 1770s. Of dark brown leather. Sharply pointed toe; a low stacked heel is now missing. Straights; straps to buckle over rounded tongue. Dog-leg side seam. From a farm at Church Brampton, Northamptonshire, it shows evidence of having been worn in the farmyard, although the sides are rather low cut.

a black satin shoe in Whitby Museum, man's size, with a 6-inch heel, which would do just that; possibly a dancing shoe. Red heels continued (figs. 18 & 21), but by 1771 they were not restricted to either grand dress or men. A *London Magazine* writer asked: 'whether your London ladies like your London gentlemen intend to wear red heels to their shoes' (fig. 24a). And there was rather more bizarre wear for men at the seaside (as today). The *London Chronicle* of 1787 said: 'Your first appearance must be in red morocco slippers with yellow heels' (fig. 28).

It was Rococo elegance and the tea table which civilized the English and made massive jack boots with wide tops unacceptable in a drawing room. In

1731 'Top Boots' Tottenham, who rode all night to reach the Irish parliament for a critical division, entered the House still wearing dirty riding boots, and was heavily fined for doing so. His 1731 portrait by James Latham in Dublin shows jack boots with clumsy top, fitting the thigh.

SHOES
Shoes therefore became the dominant wear, with the buckle set high on the instep at first, the side seam usually angled, without the occasional curving line of the early part of the century. In 1745 J. Martin in the *Art of Cordwaining* mentions 'long quarters' (fig. 21), and they became more common from the 50s. In the August 1755 *London Magazine* there is a refer-

24 Women's buckle shoes, clog and French mule, 1720s-30s. (a) Of green, pink, yellow and white floral silk brocade. Needlepoint upcurved toe, 2-inch red morocco covered heel. White kid rand; straights. White finish under arch; straps to buckle over high tongue. Matching clog with the same toe. Straps lined with red flannel, ribbon tie. (b) Of cream, with blues, greens, pink and gold floral silk brocade, 1736-42. Blunt pointed toe. 1.8-inch covered heel. White kid rand; straights. Star stamps on sole and traces of white finish under arch. Straps to buckle; brown leather insole. Silver braid up back of heel, and originally also centre vamp. (c) Mule of rust silk damask. Long pointed toe, 4-inch covered heel. White kid rand; straights. Peaked vamp; half sock of brocade, with vandycked edge. Silver braid at centre vamp and back of heel. French style, for salon wear.
▽

ence to 'buckling just above the toes' — though this was not to become general until the 70s. *Town and Country Magazine* in 1772 said the following on macaronis: 'The shoes are scarce slippers and their buckles are within an inch of the toe . . . cut like a butter boat to show the clock of the stockings'. We are told that in Virginia in 1772 'the gentlemen now call frequently for shoes with long hind quarters and that buckle low on the foot.' The whole shoe became lighter, although some had been lighter from the 50s. *Monsieur à la Mode*, 1753, says: 'a pair of smart pumps made up of grained leather, so thin he can't venture to tread on a feather.' Footmen too wore light pumps.

For the labourer, the style was the same, but with heavy hobnails where required. Metal 'horseshoes' for heels occurred as early as 1748. P. Kalm, *Account of his visit to England*: 'the shoes which the labouring man commonly used . . . were strongly armed with iron. Under the heel was set an iron which followed the shape of the heel and somewhat resembled a horseshoe. Round about the soles were nails knocked in quite close . . . also knocked full of nails under the middle of the sole.' The cost of a pair of shoes was high in proportion to a week's wages. Nonetheless, though there are many illustrations of poverty, few show the English barefoot, other than children who naturally prefer that condition. Where different conditions prevail underfoot, i.e. Scotland, Wales, Ireland, there are more barefoot adults, but anyone who has walked through bogs in wet shoes will understand.

BOOTS

Boots from the 1720s onwards were relegated to riding or military use. The heavy Marlborough-type jack is still illustrated in Diderot's *Encyclopédie* and Garsault's *L'Art du Cordonnier* in the 60s. It became rarer in Britain, although a postboy of 1774 is shown in the Bunbury print 'Courier Anglois' on horseback in a rigid leg jack boot, like fig. 22, but undecorated. Postillions continued to wear heavy boots for protection, double-cased and virtually indestructible, but these were made obsolete by coaches in the 1820s. By 1800 the pass line was cut very wide, to enable a shoe to be worn inside. Gambadoes continued, serving the same purpose of protection and insulation.

By 1727 the riding boot leg had become softer and closer fitting; see the John Wootton painting of the racehorse Smiling Ball formerly in the possession of Messrs Spinks, with his jockey in close-fitting boots with brown top. With the growing interest in horse-racing, the light jockey boot became important. The

top was turned down below the knee for greater mobility, showing the brown lining. It was soon adopted as fashionable wear. *Universal Spectator* of 1739 mentions 'a set of sparks who choose to appear as jockeys, seldom to be seen without boots.' There are more references to the booted look for walking in the 70s when they really became fashionable (fig. 20), a reflection of the war, and continued into the 80s: General John Burgoyne's *The Lord of the Manor*, 1780, mentions 'Young fellows so fond of boots at all hours except when on horseback. Then nothing but a white trouser . . . and a pair of dancing pumps.' La Rochefoucauld, *Mélanges sur l'Angleterre*, on life in English country houses, 1784, says: 'In the morning you come down in riding boots and a shabby coat.' If you look like your groom, there is less problem of a revolution. These are the boots with brown top featured in caricatures of John Bull, the nearest an Englishman has come to national dress. By the 80s they were worn with great swagger with mock straps dangling outside, while the real loops for pulling on were hidden inside. The top boots worn by Thomas Jefferson, now in the Smithsonian Institution, are of this type, but have the oval toe of the end of the eighteenth century. Military boots with top turned up over the thigh continued, narrower now and the top cut away behind the knee by the 40s; see the 1742 illustration of Life Guards.

There were also half boots from the 1750s, cut a little higher than modern ankle boots, which descend from them, and worn for shooting and by the military. *St James' Chronicle*, 1763, comments on 'tradesmen who ape their betters . . . breeches almost met by a pair of shoes that reached about three and a quarter inches above the ankles.' They were typical wear for both sides during the American War of Independence (see Peale's portrait of Captain John Harleston of Chicago, 1776).

SLIPPERS

Indoor slippers continued in mule form, cut lower from the 1730s; see Hogarth's *The Rakes Progress II*, 1733, the rake in undress. At first of brocades, they changed to light leathers in assorted colours. Tristram Shandy, 1766, appeared in 'a yellow pair of slippers' (Eastern influence here?). From the 70s they were cut even lower, but with a tabbed front, which had occurred intermittently from the 30s, a style later to be christened Albert.

If all this sounds dull in comparison with the richness of men's clothes (fig.23), it is because all decoration was channelled into the buckle. Worn by both sexes, they began to grow in the 1730s and again in the 60s, culminating in 1777 in the Artois buckle (a quite defiant fashion to choose in war). Their sheer size necessitated modified chapes, and false straps were mentioned by 1787. They were as dangerous as they look. Lady Mary Coke related of Lady Bridget Lane at a royal ball in 1767 that 'Her shoes were fastened with an embroidered rose of her own work, which catched in the Duke of Gloucester's buckle and pulled one of them off in the middle of the dance.'

But the glittering paste was beginning to look out of place with the shabby coat attitude of the late 80s, so that on 31 May 1788 the *General Evening Post* says that 'the massy Artois buckle seems giving place to the shoe tie, which are surely lighter and more elegant, at least for morning undress' (plate 2c). And 'down with the aristocratic shoe buckle!' was to be a cry of the French Revolution, summing up, as it did, all the wealth and ostentation and sheer inconvenience of high fashion. The revolution killed the fashion for buckles, so that 20,000 bucklemakers were out of work in Birmingham. In December 1791 'bucklemakers . . . waited upon the Prince of Wales with a petition setting forth the distressed situation . . . in buckle manufacture, from the fashion so prevalent of wearing shoe strings instead. H.R.H. promised his utmost assistance by his example and influence.' Buckles became regulation court wear, but not even Prinny could bring back the carefree mood of ostentation that made them fashionable for all.

WOMEN'S

COLOUR AND MATERIALS

For women's shoes, the chief materials were silk and wool. The heavy Baroque velvets and silk brocades of the early eighteenth century gave way to lighter brocades and plain satins in the 1760s and 70s. Two colours were fashionable, ivory plus one matching sash or hat ribbon (plate 2a). There were textured, woven spot silks in the 70s and 80s, and linen for summer wear. Wool, alias calimanco etc. was a cheaper, hardwearing material for lower class and winter wear, and many survive, mud-spattered, with contemporary patches which no lady would have worn. They were mostly lined with kid, usually white, though very few had leather as the outer material of the upper until the 80s (fig. 25), when materials for men's and women's shoes became very similar: another sign of the move towards equality. Lady Mary Coke did fall for French painted leather shoes which she saw in Belgium in 1767, and sent home half a dozen pairs (there are such shoes in the Victoria and Albert and Keigh-

ley Museums), but they were not common. There were a few suede shoes in the 80s.

With the use of so much cloth, one might reasonably have expected shoes to be made of the same material as the dress, but this was very rare. Joseph Nollekens's bride at her wedding in 1772 had 'shoes . . . composed of the same material as her dress, ornamented with silver spangles and square Bristol buckles, with heels three and a half inches in height.' It was and still is a nuisance to have to search for matching shoes, except for special occasions. There are surviving examples of dress and matching buckle shoes in the Wadsworth Athenaeum, Hartford, and in the Smithsonian, Washington, both of c.1780. Some fur was used for winter. The white kid rand continued, but died out in the 60s (fig. 24).

The plainer materials were not left plain, and braiding continued to c.1750 (figs. 24b & c), worn by most levels of society. Defoe's country girl in *Everybody's Business, Nobody's Business*, 1725, going into service in London: 'her neats leathern shoes are now transformed into laced ones with high heels.' Purefroy in *Letters*, 1744, requests 'enough of fashionable silver lace to lace four pairs of shoes for my mother, and a yard of narrow silver lace to go up the seam behind the shoes.' It was then replaced with embroidery and spangles (plate 2b & c). 1763, *London Chronicle*, for a wedding: 'silver spangled shoes'. Fanny Burney's Christmas present from the Queen, 1786, was: 'two pieces of black stuff very prettily embroidered for shoes'. The *Lady's Magazine* began to include embroidery patterns for shoe vamps, e.g. in June 1777 'two new and elegant patterns for shoes, one for gold and silver, the second for foils.' With the increase in the number of women shoemakers in the eighteenth century, some were probably encouraged to take up embroidering vamps. There is a book in Norwich Museum of such patterns, the earliest dated 1779, 'Drawn from the *Lady's Magazine*', with the name Sophia Hase. At a lower level, there are cloth-topped shoes which have been re-covered in black for mourning, with painted heel, which was otherwise beyond an amateur's skill. The majority of surviving shoes in old American collections are of French or English manufacture until the 1790s, when some smart ones began to be made at Lynn, Massachusetts and Philadelphia.

TOES

Like the men's, the women's toe was sharp and upcurved at first, blunter in the 1760s. The *British Magazine* of 1763 says: 'the flat-heeled drudges now are thrown aside, for the high pumps with toes of peaked pride.' They became sharp again, though no longer upcurving in the 70s, with matching pointed tongue (plate 2b). In 1778 a lady ordering shoes for Bedford Races asked for them: 'not so round at the toe'. About 1786-7 there was a brief fling of sharply upcurving toes, linked with the vogue for Chinoiserie. The *Ipswich Journal* of 1787 refers to the 'Kampskatcha slipper of fine black Spanish leather and turned up at the toes in the Chinese taste' (fig. 25).

HEELS

The high, thick Baroque heel continued to the 1760s, though rather more curvy on the back line than in 1700. The construction was still the louis, christened Louis XV in the 1860s (fig. 35.3). These thick heels were not worn in France and Italy, though they were almost as thick in Holland and Germany. The French or Pompadour heel, from c.1720, was much more slender, if not positively flimsy (fig. 24c), adequate for salon life, as in De Troy's oil, 'Reading from Molière', 1728. They were occasionally found in England as the century progressed. *Receipt for Modern Dress*, 1753, advocates: 'Mount on French heels when you go to a ball, 'Tis the fashion to totter and show you can fall.' In 1762 the *London Chronicle* says: 'As to their shoe heels, ladies go just as they did, some as broad as a teacup's brim and some as narrow as the china circle the cup stands on.' There were more references to French heels in the 80s. Cowper's country lass in *The Task* is 'ill-propped upon French heels.'

By the later 60s the slender heel gained favour, known as the Italian heel, wedged to support the arch (plate 2), which had only a leather shank. In August 1776, *Gentlemen's Magazine* said the following about the Modern Belle: 'Heels to bear the precious charge, More diminutive than large, Slight and brittle, apt to break, Of the true Italian make.' Some were made impossibly thin, of wood under the fabric covering, requiring a metal spike like the 1960 stiletto heel. Such trifles would have been quite impractical to wear on uneven cobbles and demanded level pavements.

By the later 80s heels were again becoming more practical, suiting the leather uppers (fig. 25b), with the subconscious fear of a possible revolution. Sophie von La Roche writes in 1786 of London maids: '. . . nearly all the women wear black shoes with very low heels when walking'.

As on the men's shoes, the side seam moved nearer the toe, the whole appearance growing lighter. Francis Fawkes in *His Mistress's Picture*, 1755: 'Mounted high and buckled low, Tottering every step they go'.

OVERSHOES

The overshoes obviously had to be modified to fit, with the same toe shapes. The fitted clog (fig. 24a) continued throughout the period, though the arch and heel socket were modified. There were galloches too, with rather more upper. In 1737 'Galloche means a sort of slipper worn over the shoes'. A 1764 advertisement in *Northampton Mercury* was for 'Black leather clogs 2 shillings 6 pence. Toed clogs 3 shillings 10 pence.' As late as 1786 the Queen advised Fanny Burney to put on her clogs to deliver a letter one October evening. In 1785 Alexander Gillies took out a patent for sprung clogs: a toe cap with forepart sole, with or without latchets, and a kid-covered spring loop to hook round the heel — again unthinkable before pavements.

Pattens were generally relegated to lower class and country wear. Of Defoe's country girl going into service in London in *Everybody's Business, Nobody's Business*, 1725, we are told: 'Her high wooden pattens are kicked away for leather clogs.' By 1774 pattens were found to have their uses, even by aristocratic ladies: Lady Newdigate-Newdegate said, on Buxton 'The way to the well was almost impassable. We have been forced to get high pattins and with them do vastly well.' Elizabeth Noel, writing from Bath, said: 'I have asked for cloak . . . and pattens, and then I shall be properly equipped to sally forth.' In 1 December 1789 Betsy Sheridan also says on Bath 'We ladies here trot about in pattens, a privilege granted nowhere else to genteel Women.' It can be very wet in Bath.

The Buxton lady talks of high pattens, and they were as much as twice as high as the nineteenth century version. The coloured engraving, 'Piety in Pattens', 1773, shows a housemaid with mop and bucket in high-heeled shoes, with flat-soled pattens (a new development in place of the wedged arch) strapped under them, with a high, almost circular iron. One of them survives in the Cambridge Folk Museum. All have pointed toe.

BOOTS

With the men's craze for boots for walking, it is not surprising to find them being worn by women as well, from 1778, though chiefly for riding and driving, calf-high kid, front lacing, with fashionable toe and Italian heel. The *Ipswich Journal* of 1786 says that 'the ladies begin to wear Morocco half boots and Hussar riding habits'.

The Industrial Revolution had no effects on shoe making as far as mechanization was concerned, but it did affect production methods. By 1764 in a

Northampton Mercury advertisement prices were quoted for bespoke and ready made, men's and women's shoes at about 5 shillings bespoke, and 9 pence cheaper for ready made. So more shoes were inscribed with the customer's name, on the quarter lining, or occasionally under the vamp.

Shoemakers began to advertise with trade cards (from at least 1733), and from c.1750 with labels on the sock. Northampton Museum keeps a card index of shoemakers, which can never be complete, but is available for consultation: it gives dates when shoemakers were active, with biographical details as available. The labels suggest not just mass produced 'ready mades', but also pride of workmanship, which was so patently justified when the shoes are examined. Oliver Goldsmith's *Citizen of the World*, 1761, comments: 'Englishwomen's feet are ten inches long — an acceptable size today. So perhaps surviving shoes are deceptive.

---

25 Women's shoes in the Chinese taste, 1786-7. (a) One of a pair of green leather. Very narrow, pointed upturned toe; $1\frac{5}{8}$-inch white kid covered sturdy heel, slightly wedged. Straights; drawstring through top edge binding; hessian lining. (b) One of a pair of strong black leather. Sharply pointed prow toe, over oval sole; $1\frac{1}{8}$-inch covered wedge heel. Brown leather rand, white stitched. Thick sole; straights. Ring stamps on sole and brown edge finish under arch. Tan kid quarter lining, with red morocco grip at top back. A substantial, almost waterproof construction, contrasting with the impractical low cut and fashionable toe. The shoes show signs of wear.

4
1790-1830
Regency to George IV

This period was dominated by the Napoleonic Wars and their aftermath, by the Prince Regent/George IV, with Beau Brummel in the early years, Neo-Classicism, followed by Romanticism. It was a time of great upheaval, with fears of revolution and invasion, and a massive war effort. There was a brief flirtation with machinery for making army boots from 1810 to 1815, invented by Marc Isambard Brunel, using a riveted construction. The urgency of producing boots quickly with unskilled labour ceased; the boots were inferior and rigid, quite out of keeping with post-war feeling, and when the factory was damaged by fire, the method went out of use, until revived by Crick in 1853. Is it just coincidence that riveting was the Roman method of construction and this is a Neo-Classical period? Brunel may have got the idea from studying ancient styles.

MATERIALS
There was quite a lot of other metal in footwear, in tune with the martial spirit of the times. Cruikshank's satirical print, 'Shoeing Asses, or the Present Fashion of Making Boots Everlasting' published in 1807, comments on the steel tips and heels for dandies' boots. They were also used on workmen's hob-nailed high-lows. Scott's *Waverley*, 1814, speaking about 1805, says: 'My hero will neither have iron on his shoulders, nor on the heels of his boots, as is the present fashion of Bond Street.' Many of the leg boots had spurs attached, built into the heel, instead of on a separate spur leather, as previously. They were worn for walking, and were especially popular c.1817-19 and again from 1825-9. Northampton Museum has a leg boot of c.1820, cut down to ankle height, with the spur built in. Metal eyelets were patented in 1823 by Thomas Rogers, though these

were only slowly adopted.

The other new material was patent leather. Peal's, established in 1791 as leather japanners, claimed to be the inventors of waterproof leather. In 1790 Thomas Saint's patent for closing also included 'certain compositions of the nature of japan or varnish', though it was too late to patent the full process of making 'patent leather' when it came into general use in the 1790s. It coincided with the craze for a high gloss, secret recipes for blacking, and rumours that Brummel's valet cleaned his master's boots in champagne. In the United States patent is said to have begun in 1822 at Newark, New Jersey.

The most important technical innovation was the re-introduction in the 1790s of rights and lefts. Shoes had been made straights since the beginning of heels in 1600. Now with a return to flat shoes, it was less difficult to make a mirror-image pair of lasts and, with the development of the pantograph in the early nineteenth century, rights and lefts gradually ousted straights, though women were slower to adopt them than men. Rees in 1813, and subsequent authors for

---

26 The Art and Mystery of a Cordwainer, *by John F. Rees, published London, 1813. Figs. 1 and 2: the patterns for uppers of men's welted shoes. This is one of the first textbooks on shoemaking and highly respected by subsequent shoemakers. The dotted lines indicate where the shoe is to be strained in lasting, and the letters refer to instructions for making. The sole and heel have to be added. 'The common height of the heels of men's shoes now is only a top piece above a split-lift.' Note the variation in type of side seam. The straps were punched to take a lace after finishing.*

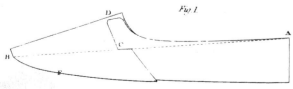
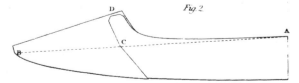

many years, discussed the pros and cons: 'If the wearer do not tread even, the shoe must wear much on one side'; and flat-footed people found rights and lefts very uncomfortable, not to mention those with gout, rheumatism and corns. Regimental standing orders for the King's Shropshire Light Infantry in 1800 were: 'Soldiers will wear their boots on alternate feet on alternate days.' The army wanted them to last longer. By 1827, *Crispin Anecdotes* records that 'Rights and lefts . . . now become pretty general.'

In the United States, rights and lefts were said to have been 'invented' by the fashionable bootmaker, William Young, of Philadelphia, in 1800. With the war, the big cities were beginning to produce desirable shoes quite capable of competing with French and English imports, though on the other hand, some found the native Indian work attractive, as indeed it is. Some is almost indistinguishable from contemporary white man's designs. Mrs Simcoe's diary, Quebec, 26 April 1792, has a note about sending moccasins for her daughter in England: 'Indians do not come to town so often as they used to do . . . those I bespoke were to be much prettier colours. I think them pretty for little children in the house, but I should be afraid if older ones wore them, their feet might be too large ever to wear the Duchess of York's shoe.'

As the period began in the atmosphere of revolution, there was a natural swing to boots, for fashion, as well as army wear, and for women too. More of the women's shoes were made of kid leathers (figs. 31 & 32), instead of cloth. Northampton Museum has a wedding shoe of white kid dated 1791, with very low heel; the whole appearance is more practical. Men discarded their buckles and adopted the latchet tie of the revolutionaries. It was no longer prudent to wear ostentatious buckles and quite out of keeping with the spirit of equality, though there was some compensation in wearing less substantial leathers,

27 *'The Cloakroom, Clifton Assembly Rooms', by Rolinda Sharples, in oil, 1817. While most of the young men wear plain black lace pumps, suitable for dancing, one in a military uniform wears black hessians, and another, possibly also in uniform, has unusual pale tan hessians with silk top binding and low red heel. The ladies are shown in low-heeled shoes, white or green, which do not appear to match anything else they wear. The most interesting detail is the maid (in plain black shoes) removing her lady's cosy red ankle-high overshoes (with black furry edging), revealing the white evening shoe inside; the vamp is quite high cut, with ribbons crossing round the ankle.*

△

28 One of a pair of men's red leather shoes, c.1790. Pointed toe, ½-inch covered heel, white stitched. Straights; ring stamps on sole. Long quarters with two pairs of lace holes, each with separate ivory silk lace, matching the ivory top edge binding. White kid sock and strap lining. From Antony House, Cornwall. Possibly for seaside wear.

scarcely distinguishable from the women's. Sir Nathaniel Wraxall in his memoirs: 'Dress never totally fell till the era of Jacobinism and of equality in 1793 & 4. It was then that pantaloons, cropped hair and shoe strings, as well as the total abolition of buckles and ruffles . . . characterized the men.'

29 Men's boots. (a) One of a pair of top boots of black leather with matt fawn-white top. Square toe, ¾-inch stacked heel with very fine rand wheeling. Not straights; ridged shank. Small multi-ring stamps on sole; pointed vamp. Mock strap stitched down on outside top and back. Pair of canvas straps inside to pull on. About 23 stitches to one inch. c.1810-20s. (b) One of a pair of dress wellingtons, black patent leather golosh, maroon leather leg with olive top binding and lining (marked by decorative stitching centre front). Square toe, 1-inch stacked heel; not straights. Wheeling and finishing under arch. Leg has side seams only, with bead. Canvas straps inside to pull on. c.1817-20s.

▽

a   **b**

In the United States buckles persisted. George Washington's 1796 portrait by Gilbert Stuart shows him wearing large silver buckles with gilt studs, and as late as 1829 Pat Lyon, the blacksmith in John Neagle's portrait also wears silvery buckles.

TOES

With this period of turmoil too there was an enormous choice of basic shapes. The toes began pointed, but were succeeded by or worn side by side with a blunter oval (figs. 31a & b). Princess Sophia's court shoe of 1796 still has a needlepoint toe, while a wedding shoe of the same year is oval. From 1817 the oval also competed with a square toe, which gradually became dominant after 1825 (fig. 29b). There is an American oil painting, 'Country Wedding', by Krimmel c.1819, with the bridegroom already in square-toed lace shoes.

HEELS

Heels had their ups and downs too. The men's disappeared completely in France in 1789, until men complained that heels were necessary to anchor the trouser strap. They were commonly 'a top piece above a split lift' (Rees, 1813), but most of the surviving examples show a ½ to 1-inch heel, mostly decreased to very short from back to front (fig. 29b). There were a few boots with high heels for dandies, as is testified by one of c.1819-20 in Northampton Museum with a 2½-inch heel and a narrow domed shank beneath a highly curved arch. The women's ranged from the thinnest of stilettos derived from the Italian heel; the Bowles & Carver print of 1797, 'The Fashionable Shoemaker trying on an Italian Slipper', shows him removing a buckle shoe and offering a slipper with peaked vamp and thin Italian heel. There were arched wedges (fig. 32b), true wedges (fig. 32a), stacked, or single lifts (christened the Duchess of York in 1792) (plate 3), and everything from D-shaped to crescent top pieces, until the heel disappeared completely in the 1820s (fig. 32c). In Northampton Museum there is a lavender silk shoe with square toe and throat and ribbon ties, by Melnotte of 1827, which is heel-less.

MEN'S

BOOTS

For men boots naturally predominated until about 1820. Captain Gronow's *Reminiscences on a party at Manchester House* in 1816 state: 'I went there dressed à la Française with . . . black trousers, shoes and silk stockings' — a style soon adopted by the Prince

Regent. The new regulations for ball nights, c.1818, for the Bath Assembly Rooms were: 'No Gentlemen in boots or half-boots to be admitted.' Brummel's morning dress, according to Captain Jesse, was 'similar to that of every other gentleman — Hessians and pantaloons or top boots and buckskins.' The top boot became the trade mark of the English, but was practical only with breeches, and gradually reverted to a riding boot, as trousers ousted breeches for general wear. They frequently had false straps for decoration on the top (fig. 29a), though by 1809 according to the *Morning Post*, writing of the Four-in-Hand Club: 'Boots very short, with long tops, only one outside strap to each and one to the back: the latter being employed to keep the breeches in their proper longitudinal shape.'

Brummel's other choice was the hessian, cut with a V-dip at centre front with tassel; according to Rees it was 'brought into this country from Germany in the beginning of this war about 1794 or 5,' — though

---

30 Men's shoes, 1820s. (a) One of a pair of white kid. Narrow rounded toe, ½-inch wedge covered with red morocco. Straights; latchets to tie over instep with two pairs of lace holes and ribbon lace. Remains of blue silk lining. Made by David Taylor, Boot and Shoe Maker to His Majesty (at 30 Bond Street until 1819, then 12 Clifford Street, London). He also made for the Prince Regent and the Duchess of York. The shoe is inscribed with the customer's name 'Earl Shrewsbury' and 'add one inch to the length' — the side seams have been let out. For dress wear, or possibly the 1821 coronation. (b) Of black leather. Oval toe, one-lift heel. Right foot. Double ring stamps on sole. Narrow straps to take a small buckle. Silk edge binding. Yellow leather sock and part lining; the rest of orange silk. Maker's label on sock: 'Doggett & Taylor, Boot and Shoe Makers to the Duke of Gloucester, Davies St, Berkeley Square, London' (in directories from 1814 to 1863). c.1827.

one of the MPs in the painting of Pitt's Address to the Commons in the previous year also wore them, in black, with red top binding. Rees also referred to them as 'the Hessian or Austrian boot: lately, they were of a gradual sweep in front and with a peak behind; now [1813] they are square in front, and without a peak behind.' The walking attire of John Horseman in 1804 was 'hessian boots with immense tassels' (and see fig. 27). By 1830 the *Whole Art of Dress* by a Cavalry Officer says that they were 'only worn with tight pantaloons', and by 1861 Whyte Melville's *Good for Nothing* says: 'There are no hessian boots now' — though they did survive for military wear.

The hessian was ousted by the wellington. As with the top boot, the decoration at the knee was a nuisance under trousers. So the top was cut straight with a simple binding to form the wellington (fig. 29b). It made its appearance by 1817 in a Northampton price list at £1 5 shillings, or long at £1 8 shillings. (Hessians were £1, regents 18 shillings, bluchers 14 shillings and short at 12 shillings.) Wellingtons were mentioned the same year in Moncrieff's opera, *Giovanni in London*, though Wellington himself was generally shown in hessians until the Paul Pry caricature of 1827.

There were half boots too: half wellingtons, some merely leg boots pulled down, making quite a swagger (one with three buttons in 1814), and ankle boots. The latter were derived from the military and labourers' boot, the high-low, of the previous period. A Newnham, Northamptonshire, account lists a 'pair of high-tops and nailed,' for various dates between 1798 and 1806, at prices from 10 shillings 6 pence to 15 shillings. Rees commented on the laced half-boots: 'not much worn at present' — perhaps not as smart wear, but Bloomfield mentions high-lows in *The Farmer's Boy*, 1801. Fosby's *Vocabulary of East Anglia*, 1825, describes high-lows as: 'a covering for the foot and ankle too high to be called a shoe and

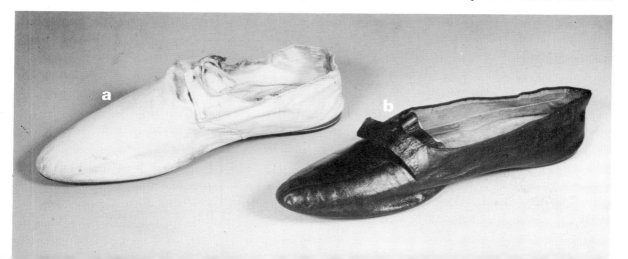

too low for a boot.' Cobbett's *Rural Rides*, 1830, says 'from the sole six inches upwards is a high-low.' Illustrations show them to be front laced, with open tab, the style known since 1817 as blucher (who fought alongside Wellington at Waterloo) (fig. 38a). They were worn for cricket by 1819, as in Henry Rossi's sculpture 'The Batsman', with eight pairs of lace holes, rounded toe, no heel. Charles Dickens recalled the street corner where he sat down on a stool c.1822-4, to have a pair of ready-made half boots fitted on. With the increased mass production during the wars, ready-mades were more commonly available. By 1830, 'with wellingtons and collegians, they are the only boots in general wear,' according to *The Whole Art of Dress*. There is a blucher of about this date at Northampton Museum with two pairs of brass eyelets, round toe, short heel, hob-nailed sole, straight side seam, no back seam, and red lined. The other half-boot, the oxonian or Coburg appeared in 1825, and had side slits, though this soon developed into the side-lace boot. Northampton Museum has a side slit oxonian with square toe, 1-inch heel and the multi-ring stamps of c.1830.

The heavy jack boot for winter riding gave way to a lighter, if equally clumsy boot, with a wide pass line to allow a shoe inside. In 1823 a much lighter gambado overboot was patented, suspended with the stirrup, with built-in spur. The roads by then were much improved.

SHOES

Although the bucklemakers' deputations resulted in the buckle's retention for court, most men turned to the lace shoe, with one or two pairs of lace holes (fig. 28). They gradually became very low cut, with short vamp and low heel, and usually black. Developed from the buckle shoe, they were open tab to begin with, though the closed tab (what we now call an oxford), which required a more exact fit, began soon after 1800. By the 1820s there was little difference between men's and women's shoes. Fanny Burney at Calais, 16 April 1802, commented on 'the women in men's hats, men's jackets and men's shoes'. As might be expected, there was some oddly extravagant footwear for George IV's coronation in 1821 (fig. 30a) and Northampton Museum has another shoe with blue-covered heel and blue binding, and there are suede knee boots for the Grand Falconer in Bath. Slippers for indoor wear, when required, were in mule form. There are at Northampton Museum some red morocco ones with yellow silk sock, and the square toe of c.1825.

WOMEN'S

BOOTS

There were boots for women, as for men, though they were not the principal wear. In about 1800 'Half boots up to the knee drawn on by means of boot hooks, are worn by many females of dashing ton' — ideal for riding and driving in phaetons. In Brooklyn Museum there is a very curious pair of turquoise leather, ankle high, with purple silk binding and wrap-over front, which may be 'the Soho new invented shoe latchet' of 1791. The riding dress in 1818 was 'slate-coloured leather boots.' The earliest were front

---

31 *Ladies' shoes. (a) One of a pair of black kid with yellow underlay, giving a sandal effect. Pointed toe, 1⅜-inch wedged heel. Straights; finishing under arch. Linen lining with white chamois grip in back. Worn by Miss Percival, sister of Spencer Percival, MP for Northampton and Prime Minister (assassinated 1812). c.1795. (b) Pale blue and black printed kid. Narrow oval toe over square sole, 1-inch wedged heel covered with blue kid. Straights; black edge binding. White kid quarter lining with yellow grip. Linen sock with maker's label: 'Edward Hogg, 25 Jermyn Street, St James's, London, Ladies Shoemaker', with royal arms. c.1796. In 1802 his labels read: 'Ladies Cheap Shoe Warehouse'. (c) Of pale blue kid, with white kid and silk appliqué. Pointed toe, 0.7-inch wedge heel covered with white kid, tapering to point at back. Straights; silk binding. Drawstring; white kid quarter lining, linen sock. c.1798.*

laced with kid leg, or linen for summer, reaching just above the calf, and with Italian heels. The heel was soon lowered, making it more practical. Emma in Jane Austen's *The Watsons*, 1804, is advised, on complaining that it is too dirty to walk: 'You should wear half boots, nankin goloshed with black looks very well.' The lace at this time was knotted inside one of the bottom holes and had a single tag, usually brass or spiral wire, to lead the lace over and over, producing a ladder effect on the outside, tying at the top (fig. 33). *Ackerman's Repository* of 1819 reports for walking dress: 'black leather half boots, front lace, or half boots, the upper part of French grey silk, the lower part black leather.' Elizabeth Grant of Rothiemurcas's *Memoirs of a Highland Lady*, 1817, mentions her walking dress: 'white gown, pink spencer and yellow tan boots with tassels dangling' (see fig. 33b, with thick sole and rand, strong enough for country wear). Rees comments

that the old kinds of clogs were 'nearly or quite out of wear . . . the cork bottom shoes and chumps [now known as clumps] have done away the use of them.' And the shoemaker in *Poetical Sketches of Scarborough*, 1813, written anonymously, offers fair Ellen, when she asks for walking shoes: 'Boots up to the knee — waterproof.'

According to the report of Berlin fashions in *Ackerman's Repository*, November 1815, 'the ladies wear demy boots — Wellingtons of red kid or morocco, or satin with yellow gilt buttons, to button at the side, or Bluchers of purple or dark blue: the scarlet in honour of the English army, the blue for the Prussian.' These were not the same styles as those which became known as wellington and blucher. The side buttons were slow to catch on, though there is a lady in a three-button boot in Cruikshank's print 'Monstrosities of 1825 & 6 (Hyde Park in Winter)'. It is a shock to find Elizabeth Fry, or Gurney, as she still was, aged 17, at a Friends' meeting in Norwich, 4 February 1798, wearing: 'very smart boots . . . they were purple laced with scarlet.' Northampton Museum has a front-lace boot, c.1820, the vamp of green kid, the leg of brown and ivory striped cloth, nine pairs of lace holes, and a spiral tag.

By now boots were becoming much more common. The bride's travelling habit in Susan Ferrier's *The Inheritance*, 1824, was yellow boots, and *Ackerman's Repository* for the same year mentions 'Terry velvet boots for Promenade dress'. So the complaint in *Crispin Anecdotes*, 1827, is not unexpected: 'It is to be regretted that many ladies should prefer the wearing of boots to the use of the shoe'. In 1829 a side-laced boot, buff-coloured, appears in Townshend's *Parisian Fashions*, a style which was to develop later.

SHOES
But the majority of women at first preferred shoes.

32 Ladies' shoes. (a) One of a pair of rose pink printed kid, with silk ribbon loops and ties to go round ankle (a sandal shoe). Pointed toe, 1.2-inch covered wedge heel. Straights; finishing under arch; silk ruching. Reputedly worn by Frances Ann Vane-Tempest (1800-65), Marchioness of Londonderry. c.1805. (b) One of a pair of fawn leather, with cut-outs bound with green silk. Round toe, 0.9-inch wedged heel; straights. Linen lining and sock, each shoe with label: 'R. Willis, 42 Fish Street Hill, London. By His Majesty's Royal Letters Patent Ladies Shoe Maker.' He appears in directories at this address 1805-17 (1818 also at 135 Fleet St, 1803-4 at 43 Fish St). c.1810. (c) One of a pair of white kid with silk ruching and binding. Blunt pointed toe, no heel. Straights; curved throat. Wide silk ribbons to tie round ankle. Linen lining and sock, blue kid grip in back. 1820s.

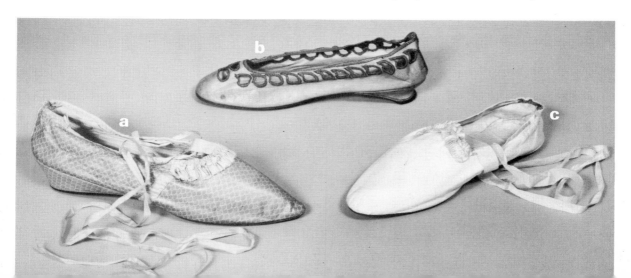

In 1792 Parson Woodforde's Nancy bought from Mr Newstead, Norwich, 'a pair of newly fashionable sandle [sic] shoes in black and yellow' (as in fig. 31a). The *New Lady's Magazine* in April 1794 reports that 'Boot shoes are still worn, but caprice is introducing a kind of sandal shoe, laced with riband, which will probably supplant the former' — which indeed it did. Rees in 1813 called them Grecian sandals. No ancient Greek would recognize them, though the Grecian sandals in *La Belle Assemblée*, December 1809, sound more likely, being 'in the form of a half boot cut out each side for lace holes'. Most of the 'sandals' were low-cut pumps with ribbons to cross and tie round the ankle, so simple that ladies took to making their own, and: 'there was hardly a lady's work table that was not covered in shoemaker's tools' (*Crispin Anecdotes*). Dorothy Wordsworth made some in 1800, as did Kitty Wellington. And the *Hon. Mrs Calvert's Souvenirs*, of 1808, notes: 'I begin a new science today — shoemaking. It is all the fashion. I had a master with me for two hours.' Two sets of tools have survived, one dated 1803 in the Museum of Leathercraft, and another with a pattern of 1818 at Aylesbury. In Providence Museum, Rhode Island, are two rolls of satin with woven designs like the late 1770s-90s vamp embroidery, imported from France c.1800 by Wellcome Arnold of Providence for manufacture into shoes. The foreign material was still coveted, but the local makers were just as proficient.

The enormous range of colours used is becoming obvious. Whatever was 'the crocodile-coloured riband' that laced the 'green morocco slippers bound with yellow for morning dress' in the 1799 *Heideloff Gallery of Fashion*? The 'geranium colour shoes for walking' — in *Ackerman's Repository*, 1826, are easier, for there is just such a pair in Northampton Museum. It is at this time that the fashion begins, which older people today will recognize, of matching shoes to gloves. *Heideloff Gallery of Fashion*, 1795, mentions 'pea-green gloves and shoes', for morning dress. White was usual for court wear and evening (fig. 32c), from 1825. But by 1823 in a Paris fashion plate, a plain black shoe appears, with narrow square toe, which was to dominate styles, and flood the English market. By 1827 the cordwainers were complaining that 'the import of French silk shoes is injurious to the sale of those of English manufacture. The Court subscribed £20 towards expenses in obtaining . . . rated duty per dozen pairs on foreign boots and shoes imported, instead of duty on value.'

There was some decoration, as well as colour. In 1796 there was mention of 'small silver clasps sewed on' — these being the last remnants of the gorgeous Georgian buckle, worn usually with a fringe. There was also ruching or rosettes. The cut-outs for the sandals were sometimes left open, but frequently in the 90s underlain with embroidered silk. There is in Northampton Museum a shoe of c.1810 with paisley leaf cut-outs, similar to decoration on dress hems.

OVERSHOES

The flimsy shoes required protection out of doors. In the 1790s there were matching overshoes with the same sandal patterns, and a spring loop to hook around the heel. Stedman in 1808 patented a flat-soled, hinged wooden version, to go with the flat shoes. Pattens continued, adapting to lower heels by abandoning the wedge, leaving a flat sole, the toe shape matching the shoes. The late eighteenth-century pointed toe patten is comparatively rare, but one survives in the Museum of Providence, Rhode Island. They were beginning to be less acceptable for ladies, though Miss Branwell, who kept the Brontës' house after her sister's death, 'almost always went about the house in pattens from her dread of catching cold'. Anyone who has seen those stone-flagged floors will understand.

---

33 *Ladies' ankle boots. (a) Of fawn silk. Blunt pointed toe, one lift covered heel inserted above the sole; straights. Front lacing over half-tongue stitched in, 14 pairs of lace holes, silk lace. Reputedly worn by the Duchess of York in 1815 (see plate 3). It measures 8¼ inches. (b) Of yellow kid with silk bow. Round toe, 0.9-inch covered wedge heel. Substantial sole and tan rand; straights. Brown fiddle finish under arch, 3 small double ring stamps on sole. Leg cut higher at back. Front lacing over tongue stitched in one side, 14 pairs of lace holes, cream silk lace. c.1815-20. (c) One of a pair of pale blue cloth printed with brown stars. Oval toe, ½-inch stacked heel. One single and group of 4 ring stamps on sole. Left foot. Front lacing with blue cord over tongue, 8 pairs of lace holes. Blue kid facing to holes. Silk ruching and rose. c.1820.*

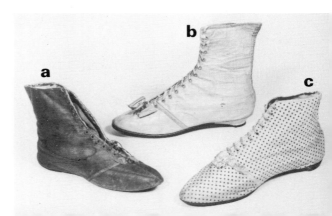

5

1830-1885

Early to Mid-Victorian

The period begins with a change from the Tory government, which had been in power since 1783, and the brief reign of William IV. Victoria came to the throne in 1837. In 1840 she married Albert, who was to dominate the rest of her life. Her reign embodies the growth of the Empire. Yet there were problems in India and Africa, and the obsessive fear of Russian expansion led to the Crimean War of 1854-6. Technical confidence was expressed in the Great Exhibitions of 1851 and 1862. Influence still came from the Paris fashion world. After the defeat in 1815, France had set about conquering her enemies commercially, as so often happens, and flooded England with French shoe imports. The problem was largely overcome by 1850. Mayhew in *London Labour and the London Poor* reported 'Thousands of ladies' French shoes that never saw France are made at this end of town.' The United States had the same problem and solved it in much the same way. Some of the New York-made women's shoes, as in London, had no back seam, in imitation of the French. And by now too, the United States may have begun to export boots, as well as moccasins and her technical innovations. Luton Museum has a pair of men's leg boots of 1839, made by Enoch of New York and sold by William MacMillan of London. This period covers the development of the manufacturing industries in the United States, particularly due to the impetus of the Civil War in the 1860s. By the 80s British shoe manufacturers were crossing the Atlantic to see the new techniques and factory organization.

There were technical changes in the shoe industry in Britain. By the 50s the sewing machine had become proficient for sewing cloth, and it was an obvious step from machining cloth shoe uppers to a machine for sewing leather, which was in use by 1856, and was little different from domestic treadle machines pioneered by Singer of the United States.

The 1860s brought the Blake, again from the United States, for sewing on soles, a machine for riveting, another for turnshoes. These were bigger, so that workers were driven into factories, and the

handsewn man battled for survival. In April 1868, the *Leather Trades Circular and Review* says 'Bespoke is generally giving way to the plan of buying articles ready made.' The account books of a Honington, Warwickshire, bootmaker, show him making footwear from 1873-95, thereafter it is mostly repairs.

St Crispin, in January 1870, described the introduction of pegged footwear as 'essentially an American institution. I shall not soon forget the curiosity that was created on its first appearance. It was in . . . 1842 that the store opened in New Bond Street . . . the window showily laid out . . . with the peg soles exposed to view'. The *National Standard* of New Jersey, 27 January 1847, had an advertisement for 'superfine stitched or pegged boots' for gentlemen. Screw clump sole boots with pegged waist were exhibited in the 1851 Exhibition, together with a range of peg sizes. They were ideal for wet wear, but rather rigid. The North Country clog too was developed for damp conditions in wool and cotton mills, using a hooked clasp first seen in the 1790s. Screwed soles were patented in 1856. The 1858 Dunkley account book has 'best calf screw clump sole wellingtons at 21 shillings.' American army boots in 1872 were brass screwed hessians or bluchers. Crick of Leicester patented his method of riveting in 1853 (a five-button balmoral boot illustrates the patent).

In 1860 another construction method was introduced, with Jeyes' patent for stitching onto an out-flanged upper, what eventually, c.1891, became known as the veldtschoen. It was not widely adopted until the later patent of 1882. It had previously only been used for repairs. There was a brief dalliance too with the cemented construction, an American patent of 1855 for applying shoe soles, and in 1858 patent cemented boots and shoes were advertised by T.F. Bancroft of Lynn, though this was not to be popularly developed for another eighty years.

Another metal innovation in the 50s was metal shanks, though not yet widely used. *St Crispin*, in 1869, describes 'geometrical bottoms — shoes with a very narrow arch'. Wildly impractical when it became

34 'The Queen and Prince Albert Polka', a print, c.1840. Victoria is in ivory satin shoes. Square toe, no heel. Tiny decorative bow and ribbons to tie round the ankle. Albert wears black patent leather shoes, very similar in style without the ribbons, and with a small metal buckle instead of the bow on the front. The buckle is typical court and evening wear, but otherwise both pairs are similar to those their subjects might have worn.

The Queen & Prince Albert Polka.

very narrow on women's shoes, it persisted to c.1874, but was domed for greater support on the men's. In the United States a fashion not adopted in Britain, except on North Country clogs, was a metal toe tip, patented in 1858 by Mitchell of Boston. There were some ladies' shoes made in Philadelphia in 1869 with a silver tip, and the black tip was popularized from c.1881 by the A.S.T. Co.

---

35 'New Patterns for Boots and Slippers', English-woman's Domestic Magazine, 1867. Paris letter reads: 'In chaussures we notice demi-high kid and velvet boots, not laced, but buttoned at the side.... Bronze kid shoes ornamented with black lace rosettes; and coloured kid or satin shoes to match the dress.... And slippers of red morocco with high heels.... It is very stylish to have the boot, shoe or slipper to match with the dress, and the fashion of short or looped up skirts has rendered the question of shoes important.... The newest styles: 1. Amazon boot. The leg is of black zephyr satin... the top... a varnished calf band, stitched with white silk. The tip is of varnished calf. Fine gold tassels. 2. Elastic boot. The leg is of fine calf, and the tip of thicker calf. Silk tassels, with a bow of passementerie. 3. Spanish boot. Of reddish brown silk, embroidered... with black silk. Louis XV heel. 4. Ball shoe. Of white satin, trimmed with... gold filigrane. Louis XV heel. 5. Fancy shoe. Of blue chagriné morocco leather, with a tip of varnished calf, stitched with blue silk twist. Heel à la cavalière, covered with leather. Blue silk bow [an oxford]. 6. Du Barry slipper. Of pink satin, wadded and lined with white silk. Ruche of narrow pink satin ribbon [bedroom/boudoir wear].'

MATERIALS

Lacing hooks were patented in 1865, and in the same year ooze leather was introduced by White Bros & Co. of Lowell, Massachusetts. Northampton Museum has a man's four-button boot of brown suede of about this date of very poor quality. It became known as 'peau de suède' by 1873 (The Queen) the beginning of modern suedes (fig. 41d). Reptile leathers also came into use in the 1860s (fig. 38b). Schayer Bros, Boston, claimed to have been the first to use alligator in 1871, though the reptiles were to develop more after 1885. A new colour began with the occasional use of browns, first seen in the Henry Garland painting of the Excelsior Cricket Club, 1864, in which the boots have tan cap, quarters and instep band with white. The two colours were popular in France, shown in many boating scenes by Tissot. A Willis and Southall, Norwich, price list, c.1870, includes 'Garibaldi boots, russet calf elastic side with fancy edging, mock lace.' And the 1873 cartoon by Spy of the Prince (of Wales) shows him in brown leather lace, open tab boots. The colour was to become popular in the next period.

A more practical material introduced in 1830 was india rubber. Northampton Museum has an 'occasionning' sample of this date with a rubber-coated front gusset. In 1832 Wait Webster of New York registered a patent for attaching india-rubber soles. By the 1840s women's shoes had discarded ribbon ties for an elastic loop. Rubber goloshes initially from the United States had also been developed by the time of Pickwick Papers, 1836: 'a wery pleasant gentleman — one of the precise and tidy sort as puts their feet in little india-rubber fire-buckets wen it's wet weather.'

In 1837 J. Sparkes Hall patented the elastic side boot, which he presented to the Queen, though in his book of 1846, he admitted they had been much improved. Coming at the beginning of Victoria's reign, they typified it more than any other style (plate 4a). In 1876 Phillip Lace, of the Liverpool Rubber Co., suggested the name 'plimsoll' for the canvas shoe with rubber sole (the Plimsoll line for shipping had been agreed in 1875), though the trade mark was not registered until 1885. Rubber wellingtons were not to develop until after 1885. In the United States there were 'Arctic overshoes' by 1872, rubber golosh with felt top.

MEN'S

TOES

By 1830 the shallow square toe was predominant for men. *The Whole Art of Dress* says: 'To be anything like the fashion, they should have the toes at least an inch and a half square'. Not an ideal style — *Shoemaker's Window*, 1838, reports: 'Lord North has knobs on his instep as large as a walnut and his toes stand one upon the other.' By the 50s they were deeper and more practical. The toe spring was made extraordinarily high. *The Adventures of Tom Sawyer*, of 1876, speaks of thirty or forty years previously: 'his boots were turned sharply up in the fashion of the day, like sleigh runners — an effect patiently and laboriously produced by the young men by sitting with their toes against a wall for hours together.' The fashion lasted to the late 50s, but was retained on labourers' boots, and for specialized hill-walking and climbing. *Dress and Care of the Feet*, 1872, also comments on the boots of fifteen or twenty years ago: 'very much curved upward at the toe. Before that came the stub toes, flat in shape and with scarcely any curve at all.' Dowie in *The Foot and its Covering*, 1861, shows an army blucher with a one-inch toe spring, and the *Gentleman's Magazine* for 1869 has black button boots still with the shallow square toe. In the 60s, the square corners were generally rounded off, a tendency which had started by 1848 on a pair of wedding wellingtons in the Royal Scottish Museum (and see fig. 37a).

36 *'Work', by Ford Maddox Brown, in oil, July 1852, painted in Hampstead. The navvies, young and old, wear open tab, front lace blucher boots in a brownish colour, calf-high, with the lace tying round the leg. The gentlemen watching (Thomas Carlyle and the Rev. F.D. Maurice) are in black, closed tab boots, probably elastic side. The smart lady wears a black ankle boot with peaked cap, probably side-lace, while the chickweed-seller and ragged children are barefoot.*

The impression of discomfort is probably correct. David Copperfield, in the book by Dickens, says: 'Within the first week of my passion [for Dora], I . . . laid the foundations of all the corns I ever had. If the boots I wore could only be produced and compared with the natural size of my foot, they would show what the state of my heart was . . . might be placed in any collection of instruments of torture'. From 1876 there are hints of the pointed toe, which was to develop after 1885. Whistler working on the Peacock Room wore low pointed shoes with black silk ties more than 6-inches wide and diamond buckles. *The Gentleman's Magazine of Fashion*, 1884, says that 'Modern trousers are close and small bottomed and require narrow-pointed boots.'

The men's short heels were relegated to dress wear, and the height settled to the one inch we accept as normal today.

BOOTS

The predominant footwear, as the British set out to conquer the world, was naturally boots. *The Whole Art of Dress*, 1830, reports: 'the hessian is a boot only worn with tight pantaloons. The top boot is almost entirely a sporting fashion . . . . Although they are worn by noblemen and gentlemen in hunting, they are in general use among the lower orders, such as jockeys, grooms, butlers. The Wellington . . . the only boot in general wear.' The hessian survived longer in the United States. The 1858 patent for a brass toe bit is on a machine-sewn hessian with pegged sole, and the photograph, c.1879 of Billy the Kid, shows him in medium high-heeled hessians with front dip, but no tassel, the straps hanging outside. Devlin's *The Shoemaker*, 1840, vol.II: 'At present we are

---

37 Men's boots and a shoe. (a) One of a pair of dress wellingtons of black leather, cut higher at back, green silk binding front top, green morocco top lining gold stamped: 'Thomas, 36 St James's Street, London.' Made for Prince Albert. Narrow round toes, 1.3-inch short stacked heel. Domed shank with black finish. c.1840s. (b) One of a pair of dress wellingtons (also known as opera boots). Black patent golosh, black silk stocking leg over tan leather lining, lime green silk top. Square toe, $\frac{3}{8}$-inch stacked heel, partly pegged. The mock bow on the front ties through a pair of lace holes. Worn under trousers, it would have given the impression of a pump and stocking. c.1840s. (c) Black calf latchet tie shoe. Shallow square toe with high toe spring, ½-inch wedge heel. Small multiring stamps on sole. Braid top edge binding and tie. Leather sock, leather and silk lining. c.1850.

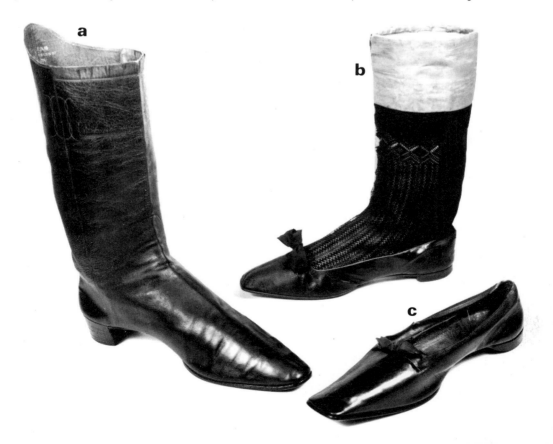

emphatically a booted people; so are the French and the Americans.' Much ingenuity was used to give **variety** to the wellington (figs. 37a & b). Devlin's prize tongue of c.1838 took the form of a shamrock. Some had legs wrinkled, with the wrinkles blocked by the 60s, though this was more usual on the military hessian – see the 1868 monument of the 7th Earl of Cardigan at Deene. Wrinkling apparatus for creasing the vamps appeared in 1864, and was used until 1900. Devlin in *The Shoemaker*, 1839, also describes the dress wellingtons: 'some have green legs, some purple, some yellow, some are made of black Spanish and some of white – grain calf, some of a sort of half and half mixture.' There were also half wellingtons, sometimes known as the Prince George.

Sam Weller in *Pickwick Papers* lists the boots he has to clean: 'hessians, halves, painted tops, wellingtons'. Also mentioned are 'muddy high-lows' and 'a prim personage in cloth boots'. Devlin too mentions cloth boots, but says: 'Nearly everybody now wears **the wellington**'. By 7 February 1850 says Mayhew's *London Labour and the London Poor*: 'Top boots are now seldom worn . . . . Boot top colouring . . . very difficult. The fashion has changed from a deep yellow . . . to a sick white.' Leg boots were revived to cope **with winter in the Crimea: wellingtons, waterproofs and fisherman's boots, and continued popular through-out the western United States.**

By April 1868, *The Leather Trades Circular and Review* signalled another change: 'The wellington . . . has . . . been almost entirely abandoned in England, in consequence of the universal use of the short ankle boot, but is still generally used by some classes of persons in the US, though in an odd fashion, with the trousers stuffed loosely in at the top.' The style is illustrated, for instance, in photographs of the 1849 California Gold Rush, though slightly peaked in front. Americans seem to have preferred the Napoleon style with the extension over the front of the knee. They appear also in the Civil War pictures worn by both sides. The cowboy boot with embroidered star had appeared by the fashion plates of 1860. But by 1848 *Godey's Lady's Book* is advocating the elastic-side or Congress boot: 'For a half century men have adhered firmly to the heavy, clumsy and un-necessarily expensive Wellington . . . . The Congress boot is cheaper, lighter and pleasanter.' There was an assortment of ankle boots. *St Crispin*, 1870, **says of** the 20s Clarence: 'one of the ugliest and most awk-

---

38 Men's boots and a shoe. (a) One of a pair of bluchers of black leather, flesh out. Narrow square toe with high toe spring, 1½-inch short stacked heel, iron horseshoe and hob nailing. Half sole repair, hob nailed. Two pairs of lace holes to tie over tongue. No back seam. Originally had loop in back to pull on. A military boot from Weedon Barracks. 1840s. (b) One of a pair of blucher or derby boots of dark brown crocodile leather. Square toe with peaked cap, 1¼-inch stacked heel. Half sole repair. Open tab, front lace over bellows tongue, with 5 pairs of eye-lets, 4 pairs of lacing hooks and a slot for lace to tie round ankle. Braid loop to pull on. 1870s to early 1880s. (c) One of a pair of open tab shoes of black leather. Wide round toe with high toe spring, ½-inch stacked heel, fine rand wheeling. Heavy sole, almost straights. Front lace over tongue, 2 pairs of lace holes. Red morocco sock and tongue lining. A combination of practical countryman's shoe with touches of the dandy: worn by John Clare, the poet, in Northampton, towards the end of his life (d.1864).

ward boots . . . blocked like a wellington, but . . . shorter and laced at the side, the opening . . . protected by a bellows tongue.' Another with side interest was the button boot, worn more by men by 1837, though *St Crispin* said 'Another boot which did not have a very long run was the Albert, connected with the late Prince. It was a modification of the French novelty.' The illustration shows a closed tab golosh, ankle high upper with five buttons. The Albert generally had a cloth leg, sometimes mock buttons with elastic side or side lace. Mayhew in 1851 called them 'Oxonian button-overs.' The early ones were flimsy. John Wright's Derbyshire account book shows a customer buying four to six pairs of boots each year during 1844 to 1850, and only two pairs of shoes in the six years: 'leather boots button 3 shillings 6 pence, Clarence boots 15 shillings 6 pence, Wellington £1 5 shillings, half wellington 15 shillings, bluchers 13 shillings 6 pence.' Similar prices are given in a Northampton bill of 1841, and in addition 'oxonian shoes at 9 shillings'. The button boots still do not appear very substantial in Courbet's painting of 1854, 'Bonjour M. Courbet', six buttons, for hiking.

The two most popular styles of the period were undoubtedly the elastic side (alias side spring, Garibaldi and Congress in the United States) and the front lace, the side lace being outmoded by the 1860s. The front lace came in two forms: first the open tab blucher (fig; 38a). *St Crispin*, April 1870, says: 'After Waterloo, Blucher gave its name to the high-low . . . Prominent in all sale shops. The back is made of one piece folded, no back seam. The laps in front are tied

through two or three holes with a leather thong, black tape or ribbon.' By the 1860s the side seam had become generally curved like a modern derby (fig. 38b). That term seems to have been first used in 1862, perhaps mock lace: the Dunkley account book lists 'side spring boots Derby.'

The second lace style was the balmoral (fig. 39c). Victoria bought the Balmoral estate in 1852, and the house had been rebuilt by 1855, and all sorts of things took its name. Sparkes Hall had exhibited balmoral shooting boots in the 1851 Exhibition; that in plate 4a is the recognized balmoral style with closed golosh. By 1855 they were listed in the Dunkley account book, for women, at 12 shillings 6 pence.

---

39 Men's boots. (a) One of a pair of 5-button boots of black leather. Shallow square toe, 1.1-inch stacked heel, fine rand wheeling. Small multi-ring stamps on sole. Cloth lined. 1840s. (b) One of a pair of lace boots of black leather. Square toe, 1¼-inch short stacked heel, hob nailed. Almost straights, half sole repair, hob nailed. Front lace, 15 pairs of lace holes, leather lace knotted at bottom, single spiral tag. Patches on instep. Worn at Hanslope, Bucks. 1861. (c) Elastic side balmoral boot of black leather. Shallow square toe with cap, 1¼-inch stacked heel. Right foot. Riveted clump sole stamped with size (8), black finishing under arch. Elastic side with four buttons and mock buttonholes. Braid loop to pull on. Made by J.W. Willoughby, Daventry, Northants. 1860s.

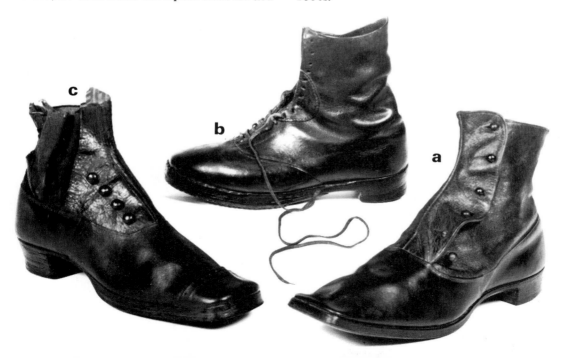

SHOES

It is interesting to see the range of styles in *Thierry's Price List* of 1884: boots for walking, four elastic side (two mock button and lace), two button, two lace. For morning, two button with cloth tops, one lace ('yellow Russia leather top, pointed toes'). For evening, elastic side. In shoes, for walking, seven front lace including five oxford, one derby or lorne, one brogue, two Molière, two button. For evening, one patent oxford, one patent dress pump. This number of shoes would not have been listed earlier. Sparkes Hall, 1846, informs us that 'Dress pumps are almost the only shoes now worn. The oxonian shoe . . . is the best shoe for walking. It laces up in front with three or four holes.' It is none other than 'high-lows now called Oxford shoes' (*New Monthly Magazine*, 1847). Latchet tie dress shoes continued (fig. 37c) and Whistler took to them when fashionable in the late 1840s, and wore them all his life, even for country walking. In May 1881: 'pink bows blossomed on his patent leather shoes'. In 1872 there was a new style. *St Crispin* mentions 'The Derby, or new tie shoe. Better than the Oxonian as the seam is not near the tender part of the foot. Especially good in summer, allows the foot to swell.' The derby (fig. 38b) was also known as the Lorne, after Princess Louise's husband, married 1871, or its French name, Molière. The lacing method from c.1800 required a single tag (fig. 39b). By 1860 it was replaced, especially for front lacing, by a two-tagged lace, cross lacing up the leg to tie at the top (plate 4b).

SLIPPERS

Slippers continued as tab front mules. In 1830 *La Mode* mentions carpet slippers worked in tapestry in a Turkish design, and a pair in Berlin wool: 'so well calculated for birthday presents and souvenirs'. The tab front became known as Albert's. The Berlin work became coarser, with lurid aniline dyes and improbable designs by the 1860s, many of which fortunately, were never made up. The cost of making up worked slippers in 1847 was 14 shillings, the same price as a pair of French slippers; twenty years later, Norris of Bedford advertises 'ladies slippers made up 5 shillings to 7 shillings 6 pence, Gents ditto 6 shillings 6 pence to 10 shillings.'

---

40 *Ladies's shoes, 1840-65. (a) One of a pair of ivory satin worn by Queen Victoria at her wedding, February 1840. Square toe, no heel. Square throat, with tiny bow and ribbon appliqué. Ribbons to tie round ankle. Linen lining and sock with label: 'Gundry & Sons, Boot & Shoe Makers to the Queen, the Queen Dowager, T.R.H. the Duchess of Kent & Princess Sophia, 1 Soho Square, London.' She wears the same style in the coronation portrait in the National Portrait Gallery. Apart from the appliqué, it is little different from most women's wear at this date. (b) One of a pair of bronze kid cameleon shoes. Square toe rounded off, no heel; straights. Sole stamped with Paris points size: 37/2, and inscribed: 4½ (English size) and 6/6 (price). Lobed vamp edged with red silk ruching, red silk binding and underlay to vamp cut-outs. White chain stitching. French import. c.1862-5. (c) One of a pair of ivory satin tabbed courts. Rounded toe, 2¼-inch covered heel; straights. Sole stamped: 'Mayer Julien à Paris' and three medals. Size 38. Gathered bow, and brass and white metal buckle stitched on front. Entwined satin and metallic braid top edge trim. c.1864-5.*

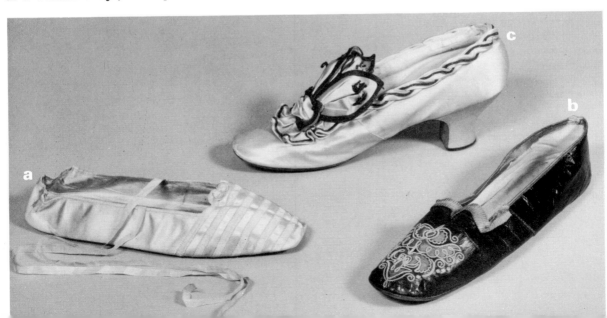

OVERSHOES

Some overshoes were worn: leather goloshes with cap and short quarters, spring strap to buckle round the ankle, during the 1830s to the 1840s. A flat-soled patten, usually without cap was preferred for country use. They were replaced for town wear by rubber goloshes.

WOMEN'S

Women had a greater choice of colours. Bronze leather shoes were exhibited in the 1851 Exhibition, remaining popular to 1900 (fig. 40b). But colours were not always welcome. *The Toilette*, 1854, advises 'Coloured shoes . . . are exceedingly vulgar; delicate pink and faint blue silk . . . have numerous advocates, but white satin, black satin or kid, and bronze kid are neater and more elegant'. From 1860 aniline dyes made a violent impact (plate 4b). *Englishwoman's Domestic Magazine*, 1862, says: 'A great revolution has taken place in the chaussure . . . . For the black shoe or boot . . . coloured ones are substituted, to accord nicely with the dresses. We have noticed some . . . in blue, violet, scarlet and green morocco. Black boots are being worn with scarlet heels and scarlet rosettes . . . but of course only on occasions when a dressy toilette is required. We need scarcely tell our readers that a boot of this description would scarcely be suitable for ordinary wear.' The colours quietened again with the Aesthetic Movement in the 1870s.

While the Victorian male may have been conquering the world in his boots, his lady was dressed at first more sedately in cloth-topped shoes, a near uniform of plain black or white satin, with square throat and no heel, designed to keep her at home (fig. 34). By 1833 in *La Belle Assemblée* we are told that 'Prunella shoes are become so common that no lady wears them.' And there are far more boots, too, side lace. In June 1831 *Townshend's Monthly Selection of Parisian Costumes* we are informed that: 'Bottines are usually made the same colour as the dress'. They were becoming more substantial too. The *Ladies Cabinet* of February 1838 mentions 'Bottines lined with fur, indispensable accessories to out-door dress'. Devlin in 1839 dared to comment: 'The handsome feet of our fair countrywomen being . . . pressed into a pair of miserable looking leather, stuff or silk . . . shoes, which in a day or two's wear, are . . . writhed into the most offensive contortions.' He mentions strong leather shoes for common or country wear, welted shoes or boots, upper of leather, spring or military heel, cork sole boots and shoes. In 1843 *Miss Lesley's Magazine* was more outspoken: 'The

insane practice that formerly prevailed of ladies walking the streets in winter with their feet chaussé as for a ballroom in . . . light kid shoes, has most fortunately subsided; and has long since been wisely replaced by . . . india-rubbers, double soles and gaiter boots.' Wright's account book lists six pairs of boots supplied to a lady customer during 1844-7, three pairs of shoes and one pair of slippers; 'cloth boots goloshed 8 shillings 6 pence, stuff shoes 6 shillings. By 1846 Sparkes Hall was advocating his elastic side boot, cloth upper with toe cap of black leather. The identical description is quoted in *Godey's Lady's Book*, Philadelphia, in August 1848, as the Congress boot: 'only about a year has elapsed since the congress boot has been . . . introduced into the United States.' But after Victoria bought Balmoral, and with the influence of the Crimean War, more substantial footwear became acceptable. *The Habits of Good Society*, 1859, says that 'It was formerly thought ungenteel to wear anything but thin morocco shoes, or very slight boots in walking . . . . The "Genteel Disease" has yielded to the remedies of example. Victoria has assumed the Balmoral petticoat . . . . She has courageously accompanied it with the Balmoral boot . . . . With these . . . the high-born lady may enjoy the privileges which her inferiors possess — she may take a good walk with pleasure and safety.'

Then in 1867 there was a hint of change back to shoes, as the *Englishwoman's Domestic Magazine* reports: 'High heeled shoes with rosettes are worn even with ball dresses'. In 1874 'The fashion of shoes instead of boots is quite a revolution in female toilets.' In 1883 'Boots are scarcely ever seen in town on well-dressed people.' Suede too made its appearance for women in the 70s, though it really became high fashion from the 1890s onwards. *Thierry's Price List* of 1884 informs us of 'Tanned swede kid evening shoes, embroidered steel beads, bows to match'. And there is a choice of twenty-two other styles of shoes: for walking, three oxfords, a Molière, a button and a Charles IX with a bar across the instep.

TOES

The toe shape, as for men's, was square and shallow. *Handbook to the Toilet*, 1841 says that: 'There scarcely exists an Englishwoman whose toes are not folded one over the other, each of these crooked and their nails almost destroyed. From childhood, the rage for tight shoes and small feet exists.' The artist G.F. Watts in *The Nineteenth Century* was still complaining about distorted feet in 1883. Mrs Trollope reported in 1832, *Domestic Manners of the Americans*: 'They never wear . . . boots and appear extremely shocked at the sight of comfortable walking shoes . . . . They walk in the middle of winter with their poor little toes pinched into a miniature slipper, incapable of excluding as much moisture as might bedew a primrose.' Frankly, the Englishwomen's appeared little better. Boots there were, but Charlotte Brontë is said to have died from cold, walking through damp grass in thin shoes. There are a pair of hers at Haworth parsonage, black prunella side lace, kid winged cap, square toe, ¾-inch stacked heel. Women were demanding more sensible footwear by 1867, as evidenced by *Englishwoman's Domestic Magazine*: 'No-one can walk well whose toes are held in a vice . . . . It is pleasanter to walk on the sole of the boot, instead of its narrowness compelling the disfiguring "treading over" on the kid. Ladies have most sensibly adopted thick boots and shoes, instead of the "brown paper" soles of forty years ago . . . . Some letters from an American friend speak of tiny Parisian shoes being much worn in New York and, jokingly allude to the necessity of amputating one or more toes to be able to put them on. There are not a few Parisiennes who have made this sacrifice.'

Devlin doubtless was prejudiced and shoes did last longer than a day or two. Every woman could make them last longer by re-covering the upper, with tiny stitches along the sole edge. Many have survived. By 1837 'current fashions demand a wide toe and low heel'. *Godey's Lady's Book* in 1849 reported 'The toes are rounded.' They had become sufficiently narrow to be described in the Dunkley account book, 1862, as 'Cashmere elastic boots, pointed patent toes.' They widened again in the 70s. *St Crispin*, February 1870, says: 'toes rather broad and rounded at the corners'. In 1880 there were more pointed toes, and in October 1881 the *Boot & Shoe Trades Journal* says: 'The present but . . . dying fashion of pointed toes was represented by some capital models of ladies' lasts, the returning fashion of broader toes by some new half round shapes.' It was the beginning of a losing battle.

The plain patent toe caps of the 1830s changed to peaks in the 60s. After the introduction of the sewing machine they were edged with a row of white chain stitching. By c.1870 there was a choice of 'fancy' toe-caps — machine-stitched designs, known as flowering.

HEELS

Though few shoes had heels at the beginning of this period, they had risen to ¾ inch by 1851, and to 2½ inches in the 60s. In June 1868, *Ladies' Treasury* told its readers that: 'High heeled boots are universal, notwithstanding that medical men have been writing very severely against them. They say the fashion causes corns, cramps, lameness at an early age, lessens the size of the calf and thus makes the leg lose its symmetry.' (Twentieth-century woman is told a high heel makes the leg look slimmer, now a desirable quality.) There was a less curvy heel from 1867, the Pinet (plate 4c), and slender stacked heels in the early 70s. In October 1881, the *Boot & Shoe Trades Journal* informed its readers: 'The latest Parisian novelty of Louis XV heels with tips showing between the top piece and the body of the heels' — which were to become very necessary in the 90s. But they were earlier in the United States. The January 1874 *Metropolitan*, published by Butterick, New York, says: 'a brass plate is usually rivetted in between the last two lifts of the heel . . . . Not only have thin narrow soles disappeared, but the small high heels . . . are becoming decidedly unfashionable. Thick broad soles and low heels have been generally adopted for the ordinary styles of walking boots.' The knock-on heel appeared as early as 1855, and there is one on a wedding shoe in Northampton Museum, and many Victorian shoes look like outmoded sandals with heel added.

Women were slower to adopt rights and lefts, and many continued to be made straights to 1900. *Dress and Care of the Feet* in 1872 says: 'Formerly, the great majority of women's shoes were made upon lasts that were straight, and the same is true even yet' (fig. 41c).

SHOES

The low sandal was none other than the 1790 shoe, now cut with square toe and throat, and heel-less. The toe shapes changed throughout the period, and an assortment of heels were added from 1850, to turn it into the 'classic' court shoe, which still exists. They were very popular. Vast quantities have survived. From c.1850 the instep was partly covered with narrow bars, the barrette (fig. 41a), or 'soulier polka' in France, illustrated for 1851 in Lacroix's *Histoire de la Chaussure*. Godey illustrated it in 1855 as 'a striking novelty in bronze or black kid cut out in bands on the instep.' It continued to c.1900.

These were too plain for mid-Victorian taste and more decorative versions appeared in the 1850s: first the cameleon, exhibited by Sparkes Hall in the 1851 Exhibition and popular by the later 50s (fig. 40b). Godey, 1855, for the morning toilet suggests 'bronze kid slipper with appliqué pattern in blue silk and chain stitch, blue satin bow.' The *Englishwoman's Domestic Magazine*, 1867, described 'Pantoufles

1 Ladies' shoes and clog, late 17th to early 18th century. (a) Of pale blue silk damask. Needlepoint toe, 3¼-inch covered heel. White kid rand; straights. White finish under arch; wide straps to buckle over high tongue. Heavily decorated with silver bullion lace. Lined with pink silk. c.1700. (b) One of a pair of shoes embroidered all over in blue and yellow long-armed cross-stitch, to produce stripes and mock braid decoration at centre of vamp. Pointed upcurved toe, 2¾-inch red morocco covered heel. White kid rand; straights. Latchets to tie over high tongue with ivory silk ribbon. Yellow hessian lining; brown leather insole. Worn with blue and ivory silk brocade clog, bound with pink, and pink lace. Leather-covered heel socket. It has the same pointed toe and star stamps on sock and heel socket as the shoe.

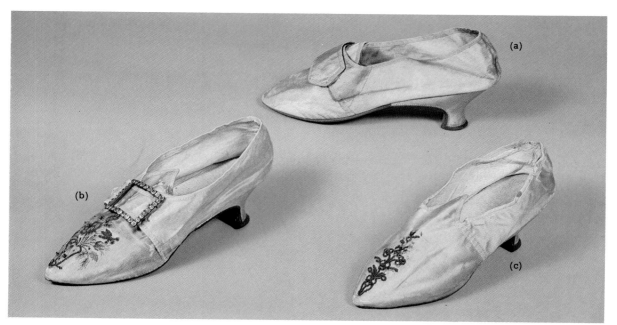

2 Women's shoes, 1770s-86. (a) One of a pair of blue and ivory satin buckle shoes. Narrow round toe, blue covered 2¼-inch thin wedged heel. Straights. Blue straps to buckle over pointed tongue, straight side seam, bringing buckle near to toe. Blue binding. (b) One of a pair of satin buckle shoes. Narrow pointed toe, 2-inch covered thin heel. Straights. Straps to buckle over pointed tongue, with original silver buckle set with pastes, pitchfork-type chape. Vamp embroidered with cornucopia of flowers in silk and silver thread and sequins. Worn by Sophia Frances Bedford at her marriage to John Pinckard, Potterspury, Northamptonshire, 16 August 1784. (c) One of a pair of satin. Needlepoint toe, 2¼-inch covered wedge heel. Straights. Pointed tongue. Vamp embroidered with silver thread and sequins. White kid quarter lining inscribed 'Mrs Burt'. Worn by Ann Bland at her marriage to Dr John Burt, Towcester, Northamptonshire, 17 January 1786. These two upper class wedding shoes illustrate the changes taking place in shoe fashions c.1785.

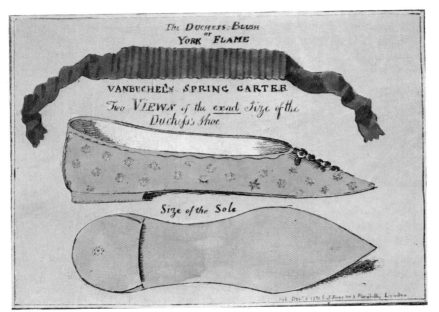

3 'The Duchess Blush or York Flame', by I. Cruikshank, engraving, published 6 December 1791. Princess Frederica of Prussia had married the Duke of York, second son of George III in November 1791 and the couple soon separated. She was noted for her tiny feet. 'Dear Miss Heber' gives it as $5\frac{7}{8}$ inches long, 2 inches wide at the largest point. There were a number of caricatures during the early 1790s referring to her. The rather bright colours are typical. In the United States, Martha Washington was also noted for her small feet, and is reputed to have worn yellow shoes to draw attention to them.

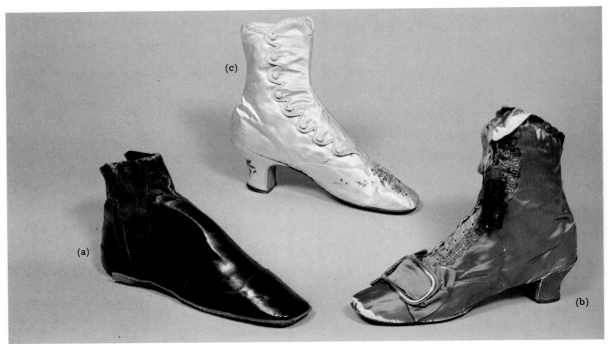

4 Ladies' boots, 1851-67. (a) One of a pair of elastic side boots of black calf kid, with patent golosh. Square toe and throat, made for low heel (unfinished). Right foot. Braid loops front and back to pull on. Made by J. Sparkes Hall (inventor of elastic side boots) and shown at the Great Exhibition, 1851. (b) One of a pair of emerald green satin lace boots. Round toe, 1¾-inch covered heel. Straights. Sole inscribed with size '4B'. Front lace over tongue, 16 pairs of lace holes, 2 brass tags. Machine sewn upper. White kid lining. Metallic braid and tassels; brass buckle stitched over satin bow. c.1862. (c) One of a pair of white satin 8-button boots, the upper hand painted with flowers. Rounded toe, 2¼-inch covered Pinet heel. Straights. Sole stamped: 'F. Pinet, Exposition Paris 1867' (where this was exhibited). The firm of Pinet was noted for hand painting and for the style of louis heel which did not flare out above the top piece. This pair was worn as wedding boots.

caméléons made in bronze and the toes ornamented with open lace appliqué. Satin is inserted under in a kind of pocket . . . . Satin of various shades is sold with these shoes ready to fit in, so with your blue dress your shoes are blue, and so on'. None seems to have survived and it sounds like the last desperate fling at the end of a style.

A second form of decoration was a tiered bow, the fenelon, added to the vamp from c.1863, and especially popular in the 1870s. Slater of Broadway, New York, advertised them in Demorest's *Illustrated Monthly*, March 1869. The Museum of London has the fenelon shoes by Melnotte worn by the Princess of Wales as Mary Queen of Scots for the Waverley Ball in 1871. The fenelon itself was often decorated with a buckle. In 1873, *How to Dress Well on £15 a year as a Lady by a Lady* advises its readers: 'Nice shoes need not cost more than 2/6, with a bow made up of any old scrap of ribbon and set off with good steel buckles, will always look nice. A pair of buckles . . . will last for ever, and improve the appearance: they cost between four and five shillings.'

The late 60s saw the introduction of the Cromwell or Molière shoe. Just as the Victorians copied so many antique styles in architecture, so this extended to footwear. Attractive buckles were introduced after Cromwell's death, but the Victorian Cromwell shoe flaunted a buckle on the front, usually slotted onto the straps, in cut steel, though some of the early ones were functional (fig. 41c). There had been jet and bead embroidery in the 60s, but by the early 80s beading had replaced other decoration, 'shoes with gold beaded toes, for a party' in 1882, being one example. These last two styles were to become popular after 1885.

There were also some lace shoes, especially the oxford, known in France as the Richelieu, with closed tab, three pairs of lace holes c.1850, increasing to five by the 70s, and like other costume, trimmed with bows or embroidery. It was to become more practical, with lower heels in the next period.

BOOTS

The vast majority of footwear was some form of boot, beginning with the side lace cloth top, the Adelaide, with patent cap, heel-less, eight to sixteen pairs of lace holes; or more substantial with patent winged cap, outside counter and ¼-inch spring heel. They survived into the 70s, as evidenced in a c.1870 Willis & Southall price list: 'Black cloth boots side lace Adelaides with leather winged cap and counter; also rivetted memel goat Adelaides.' Godey, 1854, from East Brook, New York, offers 'side-lace opera

gaiters, glazed calf vamp, prunella leg, or elastic side. Both equally popular.' In the 1840s the elastic side was more popular. By the 60s they were ousted for dressy occasions by the front lace balmoral in satins, or sturdy leather. *The Queen* in 1862 said: 'The small boots entirely made of kid, stitched in white, laced or buttoned up the front, are in the best taste. The Imperatrice boots of French satin tipped with patent leather . . . are the most convenient kind for winter wear'!

The 50s also saw the development of the button boot, which was adopted more slowly by women than by men. Lacroix in 1851 illustrated five or six button boots, with a low heel. In 1860 Godey's fashions. for spring in Philadelphia were: 'English walking boot . . . five button, French walking boot. . . front lace . . all with low heels.' But the *Atlanta Century* for the same year reports on: 'the Big Boot mania, women selecting knee length Dragoons' cavalry boots. Street Fashion. Boots a Fad. We prefer the ladies leave the boots to the horsemen. The women's shoe is far more feminine — especially for dancing.' By the late 1860s button boots were as popular as the balmoral. Both in the 60s were rather higher cut up the leg, in so-called Polish and Hungarian styles, with curvy tops and tassels (fig. 35). In 1862 J. Buckingham & Sons advertised 'Hungarian elastic side and lace kid boots'. *Englishwoman's Domestic Magazine* of 1867 reported 'Polonaise boots with rosette of cord and tassels quite high. Bottine Hongroise with two rows of buttons, also high and much ornamented. The buttonhole edge is scalloped to match'. So by February 1870, *St Crispin* stated: 'the principal forms of boots are side springs, balmorals and button boots.' There were also barrette boots, an extension of the shoe (fig. 41b). Godey, 1874, suggests they are 'a compromise between boot and shoe, and requires a coloured silk stocking underneath.' Boots always cost more than shoes. Flora Thompson, in *Lark Rise to Candleford*, writing of the 80s says: 'Boots were often bought with the extra money the men earned in the harvest field . . . obtained somehow, nobody went barefoot, even though some of the toes might sometimes stick out.'

At another level Godey defines the various purposes of different footwear, in Fall and Winter, 1876: 'Different boots for shopping, marketing and long excursions — high button boots of goat, broad soles, wide toes, moderately high square heels. For the house a low cut shoe or slipper. For church, visiting, the promenade a boot of fine white and black check cloth, or black satin with a foxing of French calf. In these the sole may be slightly narrower and the heel a little higher, the toes square, round, pointed or half round box toes . . . may be buttoned or side-lace. For full dress and carriage wear, the Pompadour or high French heel is worn . . . the uppers a plain button style of black satin, cloth the shade of the dress. Styles vary from the high sandal to the half-high, from the side-lace gaiter to the Louis XV slipper. Sandals are trimmed with buttons on the straps or steel buckles. The half-high shoes are called high-lows, Oxford ties and the centennial slipper.' And the Americans too were still adapting the native products: there is a bronze kid French-style shoe with pink ruching, with Indian beading on the toe and a bead embroidered appliqué collar, dating from the 1860s.

SLIPPERS

The fashion for boots necessitated the wearing of slippers indoors. By 1850 heel-less mules were back. (Lacroix illustrates one in 1851), though most of the English ones were the Albert. Godey, 1856, illustrates them as 'toilet slipper', and in 1859 as an alternative to the cameleon shoe for morning toilet, a quilted blue satin mule with ruching and rosette, 1½-inch heel. Dunkley's account book for 1853-60 lists wool slippers fur lined. There were more mules with heel, from the 70s onwards; Northampton Museum has one of 1879, of black satin with purple lining, pointed toe, $2\frac{3}{8}$-inch heel, ruching and steel beads.

OVERSHOES

Protective overshoes continued, very necessary with the flimsy footwear of 1830-50. This was the heyday of the patten as typified in Elizabeth Gaskell's *Cranford*: they were now square-toed, flat soled, to match the footwear, kept on by patent or velvet-covered leather straps, some with patent cap. They lingered in country districts or for use on wash day into the early 1920s. People today can still remember elderly relatives wearing them.

The rather smarter overshoe, without iron ring, was the promenade clog, listed on the 1835 trade card of Jonathan Buckingham of Ipswich, with patent cap and quarters, hinged across the ball of the foot. It also mentions india-rubber goloshes (patented 1842), which were to predominate over both patten and clog, though less attractive to women; advocated for gardening in Louisa Johnson's 1840 *Every Woman her own Flower Gardener*. In 1872 *Dress & Care of the Feet* also mentions 'high rubber boots for snow' — though these were not worn in quantity until the 1920s wellingtons.

---

41 Ladies' shoes and a boot. (a) One of a pair of black glace barrette shoes with decorative buttons. Square toe, 1¾-inch stacked heel with oval top piece. Straights; narrow shank, typical of early 1870s. Square throat; white silk lining. 1874. (b) One of a pair of white satin barrette boots. Narrow round toe, 2-inch covered louis heel; straights. Sole inscribed with size: 36/5. Knee-high leg with bars buttoning in centre, gilt buttons. Made by Bauer, Burlington Arcade, London, 1878. (c) One of a pair of Cromwell shoes of dark red velvet. Round toe, 2.7-inch covered louis heel. Straights; finishing under arch. Straps with one 'buttonhole', fastening with gilt buckle. White kid lining and sock with label: 'Henry Marshall, late Pattison, Bootmaker to H.R.H. the Duke of Edinburgh, H.R.H. Princess Louise of Hesse, H.R.H. Princess Christian, 154 Oxford Street, London.' c.1883-5. (d) One of a pair of fawn doeskin oxford shoes. Square toe rounded off, 2-inch stacked brown leather heel; narrow arch. Front lace over tongue, 7 pairs of lace holes, brown ribbon lace and bow. Made by Menhennitt, 62 Castle Street, London. c.1885.

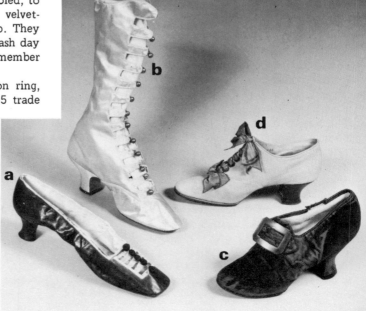

6

1885-1920

Late Victorian to George V

This period began with the closing years of Victoria's reign, the jubilee celebrations in 1887 and 1897. The Naughty Nineties hinted of the emancipation of women (they were even permitted large feet) and the practical clothes of the American Gibson Girl already far more active than her British counterpart. The century ended with the Boer War. The reign of Edward VII was brief, he who had long led society and influenced fashion as Prince of Wales. The new reign of George V was soon overwhelmed by the Great War, which saw the unequalled slaughter of the younger generation of men. Provision of footwear, on such a massive scale as the War required, almost killed bespoke bootmaking. Some survived into the 1920s, but after that only in surgical bootmaking or in the London trade.

This period, like the turn of the eighteenth century, was very much a transition, the delicacy of Edwardian design being challenged by Art Nouveau and Cubism, one style of toe shape following another and overlapping in the same disorganized way. Despite the euphoria of the jubilees and the long-awaited rule of Edward to cast away Victorian gloom, there were dark undercurrents. The pre-eminence of Paris as fashion leader was challenged by the *nouveaux riches* of the United States, and as far as shoe fashions went, it was the American imports and styles which won. Throughout the nineteenth century nearly all technical innovation in shoemaking originated in the United States. By c.1885 the 'American invasion' of mass-produced footwear was beginning (fig. 48c). It was not until 13 May 1913 that *The Economist* published an article at last entitled: 'Victory for British Boots', and the war the next year clinched the matter.

TOES

It was c.1885 too that styles began to originate in the United States, signalled by the change to the pointed toe, which was also popular in Paris. In October 1886 *Boot & Shoe Trades Journal* reports: 'Church's of Northampton manufacture every con-

ceivable shape from the dainty but cruel pointed toe supposed to be favoured by Parisian belles and beaux.' Two years later it quoted an American newspaper: 'The patent leather shoe is changing in style from a toothpick toe to a broad comfortable toe. These narrow toed shoes were producing havoc in the way of graceful walking among the fashionable young men.' Lobb sent to the 1889 Paris exhibition 'boots made on lasts in common use . . . the present fashion as worn by the nobility and wealthy classes . . . who have not given way to that senseless crippling fashion of extremely narrow-pointed toes.' They were fighting a losing battle. The September *Journal* included a London trade notice for 'spiked and medium toes'. The Americans fared better with an alternative for men of 'broad common sense toe', in the *Shoe & Leather Gazette*, St Louis, 1892. Wanamakers of Philadelphia's catalogue for fall and winter, 1898-9, has women's shoes with: 'wide, medium, and narrow English toes', the same shape as those described by Swaysland (as fig. 42) in 1905 as the continental last: 'the forepart has straight outlines'. This was the spade toe which is very much in a minority in British collections. They are mostly women's and imports (fig. 49c), though some men's were made in Northampton. The shape was superbly described in Max Beerbohm's *Zuleika Dobson*, 1911, on the Duke of Dorset's foot: 'so slim and long were they, of instep so nobly arched, that only with a pair of glazed ox-tongues on a breakfast table were they comparable.' Bective's catalogue of men's for 1906 offered three toe shapes: 'smart, medium and round'. Today we would describe those illustrated as pointed, oval and rounded. All had straight caps, as did most footwear in this period, such as the 1888 Northampton Arbitration Samples (fig. 45a). They were brogued in Swaysland, 1905.

By 1910 a new American toe shape had arrived, the bulldog or Boston (re-christened the 'bump toe' when revived in the mid 1970s) though this had appeared in the United States by at least 1898-9 for men in Wanamakers' catalogue. There is a shoe

42 'Different Types of Heels', Design and Manufacture of Boots and Shoes, Edward J.C. Swaysland, 1905. (4) Women's derby or Gibson with shallow toe, wide lace. (2 and 3) Women's and children's button boots, curved top, scalloped edge; from a Bective advertisement. (8) Women's oxford shoe, peaked cap, wide lace. (5) Women's derby boot with cap, contrasting counter and facing. (7) Women's closed tab lace boot with patent cap. Bective. (6) Women's beaded cross bar shoe. Bective. (1) Men's derby with cap. (9) Women's Langtry shoe with strap buttoning over high tab and steel buckle. Bective. (10) Men's sports boot.
▽

43 Daily Mail, 4 April 1912, front page. Manfield & ▷ Sons' advertisement. The Reliable M for gentlemen consists of four boots: Eton, lace and button bals, and derby. Note the contrasting dull leg with patent golosh on the button bal. Two shoes: a derby and a brogue. The Zephyr for ladies again consists of four boots: 2 low-heeled bals, little different from the men's, apart from the higher cut legs; 2 bals with Cuban heels, a lace and a button. 2 oxford shoes with Cuban heels, one a light brogue. All are priced at 16 shillings 6 pence, apart from The Original at 10 shillings 6 pence (Manfield was a prestige quality house). All have toe caps, though the women's plain oxford is also available without cap. Most have a choice of black or brown. The impression is of strong, almost unisex footwear.

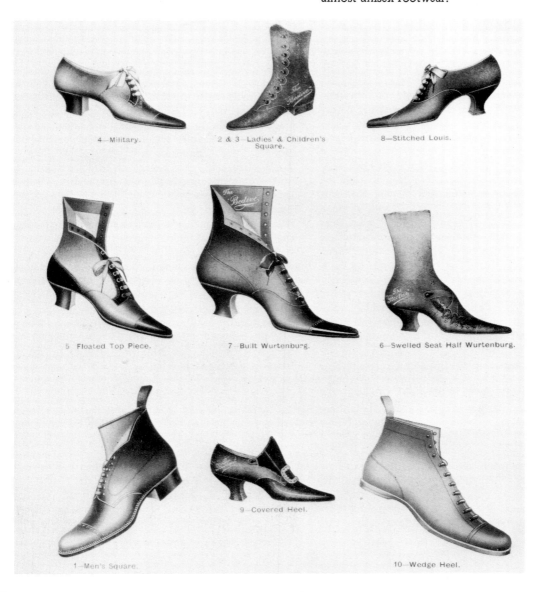

4—Military.

2 & 3 Ladies' & Children's Square.

8—Stitched Louis.

5 Floated Top Piece.

7 Built Wurtenburg.

6—Swelled Seat Half Wurtenburg.

1—Men's Square.

9—Covered Heel.

10—Wedge Heel.

from 'Moccasin', four-eyelet derby, bulldog toe with cap, suede lining, 47 shillings 6 pence, with space to pile the toes one over the other. It reflected Art Nouveau curves, combined with a sharp angle at the sole joint (fig. 47b). The Americans were kinder. The 1894 Cammeyer, New York, catalogue offered 'old ladies' comfort side-lace boots.' The set of ten Farley's samples, pairs to those on The Titanic, 1912, were all bals (balmorals): five with pointed toe,

---

44 *'Corporation Street, Birmingham', by Joseph E. Southall, mural, 1914. The toes are pointed. Two ladies wear light legged bals with patent golosh, one lace, the other button. Another wears smart shoes with wide lace. The flower-seller is in black lace boots with square toes, which look distinctly masculine. The girl wears tan (?) shoes, with thigh-length leggings over them.*

CORPORATION STREET BIRMINGHAM
IN MARCH 1914

five round, eight with cap; six black, four yellowy tan. Joseph Dawson's Northampton catalogue offered thirty toes for walking boots and shoes, all with straight caps, mostly bulldog, three spade, some narrow rounded and walled, a wider oval and a few pointed. With the advent of the War, the wider, practical shapes prevailed, though some points continued for women. In John Buchan's *Green-mantle*, 1916, Richard Hannay in Constantinople as an American is described as: 'splendidly dressed . . . shoes with a hump at the toe.'

COLOURS AND MATERIALS

The year 1885 also saw changes in colours and materials. The early 80s had hinted at russet, but now it became possible to produce a light tan 'Russia' leather, which seems to have come in with colonial troops, via India. Brown had been popularized by the Prince of Wales. The 14 May 1885 *Boot & Shoe Trades Journal*, Parker, Glasgow, advertisement offers: 'tan shoe, uppers of stout brown basils'. And the same journal on 10 August 1889 advertises 'imitation Russia leather boots and shoes in tan and maroon'. But it created problems of etiquette. The *Tailor and Cutter* of 1889 said: 'No man in his senses would walk through London streets in tan shoes and a silk sash.' And in 1893 it admonished that: 'Russet shoes should never be worn with a frock coat, and never, never, never in combination with a silk hat! To Lord Randolph Churchill belongs the heresy associated with the union of a top hat and tan shoes. Piccadilly rose in indignation'. The 1894 *Tailor and Cutter* informed its readership: 'russet shoes are correct wear with Sac suits and lounges'. Although the *Boot & Shoe Trades Journal* of 30 January 1903 said: 'tan boots [are] the correct shade for the coming season', many readers will recall Stanley Holloway's monologue on brown boots as being inappropriate for a funeral, and still then regarded as only suitable for a racecourse. Contemporary literature abounds in references to yellow or banana-coloured boots for men.

A new colour, tone(e)y red, appeared in 1919, mentioned several times in the *Year Book of Industrial Northamptonshire*. V.S. Pritchett, in *A Cab at the Door*, 1919, says that the author aged 19 left for Paris in 'a classy pair of tony red shoes — the latest colour — bought wholesale in the trade'. Appropriately enough, Golding's *Boots and Shoes III*, 1934, records that: 'during the war years and the years immediately following, nearly all black footwear was finished with black soles' (fig. 46a). It was still popular when he wrote. It replaced the range of white, cream, and browns, fiddle waists etc. used under Edward, as illustrated in Swaysland. Polished soles were to be expected in an era when the butler was expected to wash and iron laces, though they did create problems. Grossmith's *Diary of a Nobody*, 1892, describes the Mansion House ball: 'I had got on a pair of new boots. Foolishly, I had omitted . . . to scratch the soles with the points of the scissors . . . . Like lightning, my left foot slipped away and I came down.' He too, in August, for Broadstairs 'Bought a pair of tan coloured boots, which I see many of the swell clerks wearing in the City, and hear they are all the "go".'

Women signalled the beginning of their emancipation by taking to leather for general footwear, which had not been usual since the Napoleonic Wars. The substantial boots seemed even more conspicuous in dark colours under delicate Edwardian dresses; and hobble skirts or no, women kept their place in society by retaining practical footwear (fig. 43). There is a *Punch* cartoon dated 5 April 1911 showing a man and a woman dressed alike. The substantial dark boots were not worn because white was unavailable. As early as 1892, the American *Shoe & Leather Gazette* reported: 'the white canvas shoe that some of our young ladies are looking at with favour . . . was born and reared on the Coast, but has wandered away and is now found on the banks of the Mississippi as well as on the Atlantic's sandy stretch'. Dooley, 1913, hints at problems: 'women's white leather shoes were first of deerskin which turned yellow, then white canvas. The new white leather is made from cowhide.'

The new materials were box calf, in black only at first, from Massachusetts, in 1885, and suede, which now discarded the old name of 'ooze'. The 14 September 1889 *Boot & Shoe Trades Journal* reported: 'another feature was the endless variety of colours presented by shoes cut with suede goloshes, in light stone colour shades, toe-capped with patent calf or morocco'. Suede in dull greens, greys, mauve and khaki was especially popular for women just before the First World War (fig. 50b). Exotic reptile leathers were developed more for men (fig. 47b). The American *Shoe & Leather Gazette*, 1892, noted: 'Alligator leather is now greatly sought in European markets. The industry began c.1860, centred first at New Orleans, the raw skins being obtained in the bayous and rivers of Louisiana. It is now principally in Florida.' In 1893 Joseph Box exhibited in Perth a 'lizard-skin shoe for a dinner dress 42 shillings,

45 *Men's boots, 1888-1919. (a) 1888 Arbitration sample ('Best'), black leather balmoral made by G.M. Tebbutt, Northampton. Square toe with cap, 1¼-inch stacked heel. Front lacing with 8 pairs of eyelets, 3 pairs of hooks. Size 7. (b) One of a pair of button balmorals, black patent golosh, fawn wool leg. Narrow oval toe with cap, brogued edge, 1⅛-inch stacked heel. Five white buttons. Made by Thomas, 5 St James's Street, London, for Goldschmidt Rothschild. c.1914. (c) British Army infantry boot, regulation no.1, B5 pattern, of russet kip. Square toe with cap, 1¼-inch stacked heel with steel horseshoe. Vegetable tanned sole, steel toe plate and hob nails. Open tab, front lace over tongue, 6 pairs of eyelets. Outside counter. Size 8.*

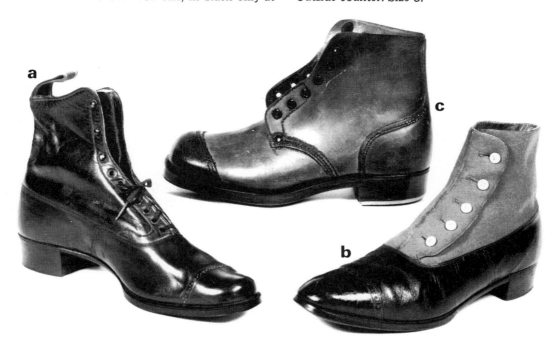

(woman's), and there is in Northampton Museum a dull green crocodile gibson of his dated c.1914, very smart, with a wide lace. Men were allowed some suede. The 7 March 1891 *Boot & Shoe Trades Journal* advertised 'tan walking boots in ooze and Russias'. By 1900 chrome tanning, first patented by Schultz in New York in 1884, had been perfected, though the arguments continued during the War as to which was better for army boots (fig. 45c). Chrome tanning won, though probably because being quicker, it was also cheaper.

This period too saw rubber as a major footwear material. Flora Thompson's *Lark Rise to Candleford* describes it in the late 80s thus: 'These new lightweight shoes in which Laura hopped and skipped when she should have walked were the thin black rubber ones with dingy-looking greyish black uppers . . . . They were known then by the ugly name of plimsolls and had for some time been popular for informal seaside wear by otherwise well-dressed women. Now they had been introduced into country districts as a novelty for summer wear, and men and women and girls and boys were all sporting their softs . . . . For a summer or two they were "all the rage".' Rubber heels became common in the 90s, and rubber soles for general wear during the First World War. Rubber knee-high boots with curved tops were patented in the United States in 1885, though were worn only in wet weather. Spike May's *Reuben's Corner*, on c.1920, mentions George Midson's new wellingtons: 'This was the first ever pair of wellington-boots in Ashdon.' They did not become general labouring wear until the end of the Second World War. Rubber goloshes were scarcely smart enough for the Edwardians, and were to become more popular after 1920.

The construction experimented with from the 1860s, the veldtschoen, had been traditional in South Africa, and was more widely adopted after the African and Boer Wars. Northampton has a man's buff oxford of c.1885-90s with this construction, and Manfield's *Illustrated Price List* c.1890 lists 'Veldt Schoen sewn or rivetted'. Otherwise, the term first appeared in a Leicester advertisement in an 1891 *Boot and Shoe Trades Journal*. In 1914 Lotus patented their waterproof double veldtschoen, which became popular in the 1920s (fig. 56a).

A solution was also found for the weak arches of women's shoes. Steel springs in the waist were certainly used in the 1880s: Northampton Museum has a lady's eight-button boot with them. They were to make higher heels more practical.

Sizes were standardized in Britain in 1885, and in the United States in 1887, though sizes had been

46 Men's oxford shoes. (a) Of dark brown leather. Kettering Joint Statement sample, 1888. Square walled toe with cap, brogued edge, 1.1-inch stacked heel. The rather heavy sole is typical of Kettering work. Black edge finish under arch. Front lace, 5 pairs of eyelets. Size 7. All the Kettering 1888 samples are black or dark brown: 2 balmoral and one derby boots, 3 oxford shoes, one with peaked cap; 2 have pointed toes. (b) One of a pair of black patent elastic gusset, mock lace. A very smart shoe made by Turner Bros Hyde & Co., Northampton, then the largest shoe factory in the world. Pointed toe, 1-inch stacked heel. White finishing on sole, brown on heel. Price on sole: '4/6'. Wrinkled front, a popular form of decoration. Back strap. Size 7. A similar pair of the same date lack the wrinkling, but has mock buttons in addition. c.1885.

a

b

stamped on shoes since at least 1780 (a woman's shoe at Northampton is inscribed 4/33). The March 1919 *Footwear Organiser* commented that women's feet were now larger, 5 and 6 being best sellers. With emancipation they shed all claims to tiny feet. Shoes had been available from some manufacturers in three widths since 1848, but it was not until now that widths were considered important, though Thierry's 1884 *Price List* had offered 'four, and in some cases five, widths to each length'. Cammeyer of New York's catalogue of 1894 offered five or six widths.

MEN'S

HEELS

Men's heels continued at about 1-1¼-inch, stacked, and it was mostly a choice of boots still, though some were more dressy than others. The elastic side or Chelsea, as it became known, declined, retained only for evening wear. Only one was listed out of a total of twenty-eight in the London Shoe Co.'s catalogue of 1894-7, twenty-one were lace (twelve closed, nine open tab), three button. *The Standard Catalogue*, New York, for fall and winter 1916-17 listed two 'Congress gaiters, for older men', eleven button boots and thirty eight lace boots.

BOOTS

Otherwise, the choice was front lace or button. The 1888 samples were all balmorals, shortened to 'bal' by 1900. Swaysland also illustrates the Eton bal, a golosh boot with open tab. By 1912 Joseph Dawson & Sons' catalogue lists 'button boots for smart wear'. These were frequently made with bal golosh of patent or glace, the legs on dressier boots of cloth or matt leather; Winston Churchill seemed to have been especially partial to them: he is shown wearing them with cloth tops in photographs from 1908 to 1916, and with the matt leg from 1913 to 1929. The 1918

Charles Chaplin cut-out doll is dressed in black patent bals with beige leg. Two-colour styles were to develop more in the next period.

SHOES

Although there were some button shoes, most were laced, either open tab derby, or closed oxford. There were superficial changes in decoration, notably the brogue, adapted from the traditional Scottish design via the punched toe caps of the 60s to 70s. In 1894 strong brogued walking boots were available, and *The Queen*, 17 November of that year, reports white kid laid under the broguing. The brogued shoe became popular c.1905, and by 1919 a Hornby & West, Northampton advertisement in the *Year Book of Industrial Northants* offered a 'brown and white two-colour full brogue with a wide lace', the effect descended from the 70s sports boots. A further refinement, also developed in the 1920s, was the fringed tongue covering the laces, first seen in a photograph of George V in kilt in 1911, and illustrated for both men and women from the 1919 *Footwear Organiser*.

---

47 Men's shoes. c.1900-1905. (a) One of a pair of oxford brogues of black Erin calf, made by Pollard & Son, Northampton. Oval toe with winged cap, 1⅛-inch stacked heel. The sole bears The Sterling trade mark with obverse and reverse of a Victorian sovereign. Hand welted. Front lace over tongue, 5 pairs of eyelets. Size 7. c.1900. (b) One of a pair of derby shoes of tan crocodile leather made by Crockett & Jones, Northampton. Narrow bulldog toe, with cap with brogued edge, 1½-inch stacked heel. Open tab, front lace over tongue, 4 pairs of large brass eyelets, wide silky lace. Curved back strap. Very sharp angle on inside waist. Tree inside.

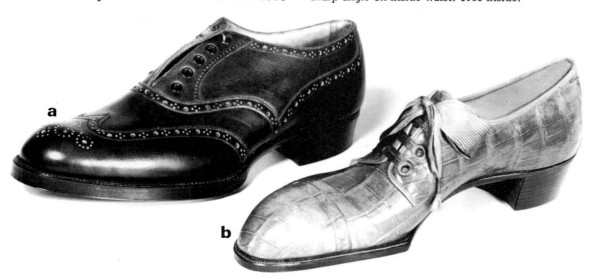

Not seen in Britain since the departure of the Romans, the sandal (a sole, with straps to keep it on) made a tentative appearance. In *Lark Rise to Candleford*, 1880s, 'a visitor in his holiday attire of shabby Norfolk suit and sandals' — and Frederick Rolfe, alias Baron Corvo, wore them in 1893. The Manchester *Evening Mail*, 30 August 1901, had a cartoon: 'The Sandal Boom', women with bare toes, a strap between the first and second toes, and ankle straps. They were popular wear for the Bohemian circle of Augustus John, and in 1907 Vionnet's mannequins in Paris had bare feet and sandals. Regarded as distinctly odd, they were not yet adopted for general wear.

WOMEN'S

As with dresses, women showed a preference for yellow shoes in the 1890s, turning to ivory satins after 1900. The *Boot & Shoe Trades Journal*, 7 March 1891, reported that 'at most of the American shops, slippers and fancy low shoes in grey and brown suede and red leather are in popular demand.' Red was worn in the Naughty Nineties, and black and white stripes (fig. 49a). Suede was to be more popular c. 1910.

HEELS

Heels rose to enormous heights in the 1890s, the highest worn measuring 6½ inches (and fig. 49b), which contributed to the exaggerated curves of the figure. By 1901 it was said that '3-3½-inch heels are decidedly objectionable; one never sees them but upon a certain shady class of the community.' Cuban

heels appeared in 1904, of stacked leather, averaging 2½ inches, to become popular c.1910. Randall's black glace bal, 1910 with 2-inch Cuban heel, cost 25 shillings 9 pence. 'Better for dancing the Boston two-step — more substantial than the louis.' Siegel Cooper & Co. of Chicago's catalogue, 1913-14 showed almost only button bals for women, with Cuban heels. In 1913 heels were decorated with

---

48 *Ladies' boots. (a) Black glace 11-button boot, probably made by Bailey & Wills, Northampton, 1888. Arbitration sample, 'Seconds'. Round toe, 1⅛-inch stacked heel. Curved top, lined with red cloth. Size 3. All the Northampton 1888 women's samples are 9- or 11-button boots, and size 3 or 4. (b) One of a pair of rust satin, covered in black Chantilly lace, made by M.E. Sablonnière, Paris, gold medal Paris Exposition, 1889. Pointed toe, 2½-inch covered louis heel. Front lacing over tongue, cord lace. Brown sole edge finish. (c) One of a pair of dark brown derby boots by Cammeyer, New York, 28 June 1893. Pointed toe with black patent peaked or 'diamond' cap, 1.1-inch waisted stacked heel. Front lace, black patent facing, 18 pairs of eyelets. Broguing. Handsewn welt. (d) One of a pair of black glace bal leg boots, with patent golosh, National Shoe Stores, London. Oval toe with cap, 2½-inch lacquered heel. Front lace over tongue, 24 pairs of eyelets. Curved top. Three-quarter back strap. Punched decoration. Size 4. Christmas 1917.*

paste, picking up the vamp embroidery. Nancy, Demolin & Co. of London said that 'our bead-covered heels and buckles are the very latest' — though the fashion disappeared during the War, to re-emerge in the 1920s.

To protect the 1890s heels, brass plates were attached by screws, usually between the top piece and cover, up to ¼-inch thick, the edge engraved to catch the light. Some were also used as top pieces, which must have been noisy, as in the 1889 leg boot by Menhennitt in Northampton Museum. By c.1918 through to the 30s, they were reduced to a thin slip of white metal, almost invisible in wear.

BOOTS
Though possibly shoes predominated over boots up to c.1910, the reverse applied later. All the North-ampton Arbitration Samples of 1888 are nine or eleven button boots (fig. 48a). The 1894 *London Shoe Catalogue* lists thirty-three boots, fifty-eight shoes, including elastic-side, button, replaced by lace during the early years of the War, up to eight eyelets and twenty pairs of hooks. One Randall boot of c.1908 has fifty pairs of eyelets. Side-lacing was also revived briefly during the War, christened Russian, 1915: 'Fawn cloth tops and patent leather fronts 21 shillings'. The leg boot had to be restricted in 1917 to aid the war effort: 'the skirt five or six inches off the ground, the height of the boot being 8 inches, and no well-dressed woman will wear a gown that covers her boot less than 2 inches'. There were con-sequently more cloth tops, frequently giving the impression of shoe and gaiter.

SHOES
There were some very high cut shoes too. The oxford/ Richelieu laced or fastened with three buttons up to the ankle in the 1890s and were hideous in the larger sizes then permitted. There is a choice of twenty-three oxfords in Cammeyers of New York 1894 catalogue, while Altman's 1888-9 catalogue has the oxford tie beaded: 'This is par excellence the Shoe of the Season, for party or dress occasions.' The

open tab derby was now named the Gibson, after the Gibson Girl, with wide laces. The *Shoe & Leather Gazette*, St Louis, offered wide silk laces as early as 1892. They were also made in white suede or canvas for Edwardian summer wear. *Northampton Mercury*, 30 June 1888, mentions 'Magpie shoes: patent black leather and white buckskin brogued' (also fig. 49a). By Tomalin's 1905 *Price List* most are oxfords — lace, button or two-bar. By 1920 it was available as a practical walking shoe with low heel.

A second style was cut high at the back with ankle strap to buckle or tie. This produced a sandal effect with ribbons criss-crossing over the instep and exten-ding up the leg, first seen in Thierry's 1884 catalogue, but inconspicuous until the shorter dresses of 1911, known as tango shoes (fig. 50b) which were all the rage in 1913, and worn to 1920. The barrette style

---

49 Ladies' shoes. (a) One of a pair of black patent courts, with white silk appliqué stripes, made by Bauer, Burlington Arcade, London. Pointed toe, 2-inch covered louis heel. Straights; black and white bow. Size 33. c.1890-95. (b) One of a pair of bottle green leather Cromwell shoes, made by Gooch, Brompton Road, London. Pointed toe, 5½-inch covered louis heel. Black sole finish. Straps over pointed tab, with cut steel mock buckle. 1897. (c) One of a pair of bright yellow satin beaded bar shoes by Brüder Lissiansky, Vienna. Long spade toe, 2¾-inch covered louis heel. Gilt embroidery. c.1895-1905.

too continued. Queen Mary's going-away shoe of 1893 was a bronze barrette with dull gold embroidery, and variants of it formed the Edwardian sandal shoes (fig. 50a). In 1915 the *Standard Catalogue*, New York, advertised an 'eleven- and five-strap sandal medium-heel shoe', the illustration for which is a barrette.

More popular was the cross-bar, a new innovation. There is in Northampton Museum an exquisite beaded white one of 1887 worn by the Dowager Duchess of Marlborough, and they were popular in the Paris Exhibition of 1889. By 1916 there were other 'fancy collar and instep designs' for button bar shoes. A simple bar was introduced in 1885, worn by Mélies' wife at her wedding, though the bar with bow, known as the Charles IX was more popular at first and was seen in Thierry's 1884 catalogue (though it had been worn occasionally from 1856). 'Charles IX' was also the term used for the barrette in Thierry. The plain bar had been christened the Alexandra by 29 June 1901, in the *Lady's Pictorial*. William Timpson's 1910 catalogue mentions 'the new smart strap shoe, Cuban heel, in colt patent or glace kid 6 shillings 11 pence'. They were to become the typical shoe of the 1920s.

Another popular shoe of 1885-1900 was the Cromwell, with tabbed front and buckle (fig. 49b). A similar style with tie instead is called the Langtry in Thierry 1884, named after the actress Lily Langtry. In the 1901 *Lady's Pictorial*, the Langtry had two straps buttoning over the tab, as it had in the 1894 London Shoe Co. catalogue. In the United States it was known as the colonial pump, e.g. 'colonial pump buckle tab court' from Walker of Pittsburgh, spring 1916. The tab with trim continued into the 1930s, though degenerating into a 'comfort' shoe,

with elastic under the tab.

And finally, there were the court shoes: fourteen were listed in the 1894 London Shoe Co.'s catalogue. In c.1900 a pair in striped satin with a bow cost 5 shillings 6 pence. Most had the bow at first, frequently beaded. The 7 March 1891 *Boot & Shoe Trades Journal* reported that 'bead embroidery is in vogue on vamps and quarters of fine shoes'. It was especially popular in Edwardian times, until the 1906 *Daily Mail* Sweated Industries Exhibition revealed the conditions which produced it: 'average working day sixteen hours, average earnings 6 shillings a week, provide own needle and thread.' Then there were more imports. Heather Firbank's account from Hook Knowles in April 1909 included four pairs of court shoes: 'violet seal, louis heels £2; the same, striped black £2 3 shillings'.

As well as the rubbers, there was a little comfort in winter too. Leno, 1895, reported that 'furred boots are very commonly worn in Russia . . . . During the last five or six years they have been worn somewhat extensively in this country . . . . Hitherto they were confined to . . . ladies.'

---

50 Ladies' shoes, 1902-14. (a) Light brown leather sandal shoe by Moccasin Shoemakers, Northampton. Pointed toe, 2¼-inch covered louis heel, with inserted brass plate above top piece. Cut-outs on front, tying over instep with wide silky lace. Bronze bead embroidery. Gold satin sock. 1902. (b) Sandal/tango shoe of black glace kid by Monquignon, rue St Honoré, Paris. Narrow oval toe, 1⅞-inch covered louis heel. Three pairs of lace holes, long wide lace to tie round leg. Cut glass trim on vamp. Lined with mauve suede, mauve leather sock. c. 1913-14.

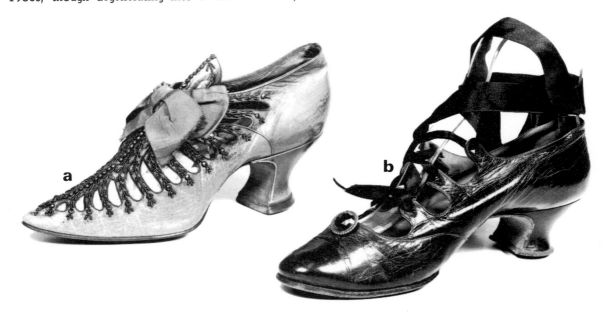

7

1920-1935

Roaring Twenties and Depression

The end of the war had brought disillusionment, due in great part to the number of killed or maimed, and the problems of employment. In 1924 the first Labour Government took office briefly, and returned to power again in 1929, the year of the Slump. Around it all, the young managed to enjoy life. Women's skirts rose to the shortest known thereto, above the knee in 1927. This was quelled by the Depression, and in spite of Art Deco, the impression of the early 1930s is of dreary clothes and shoes in various shades of mud. In the background there was still the influence of the United States, and especially Hollywood and films, the beginnings of sun-bathing, credited to a Swiss clinic in 1923, and taken up by the Riviera and California. This required more exposure of the body, and by 1931 there were open-toed shoes. 'Harvey Nichols summer suit worn with open toe multi-strap sandals.' They were introduced in Miami in 1934, and from that year there were sandals for men too. The *Northampton Daily Echo* of 20 July 1929 reported 'Two young women in Abington Street were arousing much curiosity.' They wore 'no stockings and the newest plait shoes. Bare legs on the tennis court are now quite usual, but bare legs in Abington Street are not quite so usual'.

COLOURS
Colours at first were bright. The *Footwear Organiser*, 1922, describes 'the fashion for coloured footwear and suede leathers'. Clarks mentioned in 1920: 'shoes of black glace . . . a very little dark nigger and bronze glace.' Glace was temporarily outmoded in 1924. From 1925-30 it returned, especially in pastels, and then became a back number again. Suede was popular during 1924-5, and then was unsaleable, as the adhesive used with the lining gave it a reputation for 'drawing' the feet. It returned in the 30s. But as with brown leather forty years previously, so society now objected to suede. In 1924 the Prince of Wales caused a sensation when he arrived in the United States wearing 'tan suede shoes. It was considered little short of caddish at the time.' John Taylor of the

Tailor & Cutter remarked that 'I was brought up . . . to think that suede shoes were only worn in private by consenting adults.' There was still trouble with brown too, as seen by P.G. Wodehouse, *Carry on Jeeves* 1925: 'Aubrey Fothergill . . . had been compelled to give up a favourite pair of brown shoes simply because Melkyn, his Man, disapproved of them.' But by 1935, Golding's *Boots and Shoes VI* says that 'a large proportion of men's shoes made today are brown.'

There had been more colours for men too. On 23 April 1925 *Northampton Daily Echo* said that 'Mr Churchill arrived at his official residence, No. 11 Downing Street yesterday wearing . . . boots with grey tops . . . the weather really was like spring.' The most popular was black or tan with white, a style previously worn for sport (figs. 52 & 56c). It was worn on the Riviera and there is a photograph of Arnold Bennett at Le Touquet in 1928 in two-colour oxfords. Northampton (County Borough) presented a pair of black and white sports shoes to the Duke of Kent on his wedding in 1934. Obviously a flashy shoe, it was christened 'co-respondent' by 1941, *Leadership of British Fashion*. The two-colour oxfords were also worn by women, seen for example in a Seeberger photograph at Chantilly Racecourse in 1922. They were more popular in the 1930s courts style. Mrs Churchill wore them in 1931.

There was an attempt in 1929 to keep the variety of colours for men going. The *Northampton Daily Echo* of 8 October predicted: 'Shoes for men will be brighter — there are blue shoes; very attractive they look — and quite sane . . . . They are sold, but not in this part of the world.' They were doomed to fail in the Depression. Eyelets were coloured to match the leather by 1931, celluloid-faced.

MATERIALS
By c.1925 there had been a considerable increase in the amount of reptile leathers used, especially the smaller-scaled snake and lizard. Manfield made very fine karung snake bar shoes in 1925, though it was generally used only as trims (fig. 53), because of its

51 The British Shoeman, *monthly supplement to the Footwear Organiser, May 1921. Haldinstein advertisement. Besides the Russian boot, note the gentlemen wearing spats over their boots. Left to right: ladies' shoes all with Cuban heels and wide laces — derby/Gibson with straight cap, brogue oxford, oxford with straight cap.*

high price. In 1928 Harrods carried an advertisement for 'lizard skin shoes in grey and fawn 69 shillings 6 pence, also in . . glace kid 39 shillings 6 pence'.

A new soling material, crepe rubber was used for children's footwear in 1924, and for women's the next year (fig. 53). Sole-attaching by adhesive (cement) began, c.1922, to develop for women's

Fashions in Footwear at The Grand National

(Appearing in the "DAILY MIRROR")

The Picturesque Russian Boots in Suede, and Patent Leather shewn above caused quite a sensation at the 1921 Grand National Meeting. They are designed and Manufactured in large quantities by P. HALDINSTEIN & SONS.

A regular line manufactured by

P. HALDINSTEIN & SONS

Makers of Fine Footwear to the Wholesale trade

NORWICH, England.

The Shoes shewn above will be ready for delivery before Whitsuntide.

shoes more in the 30s (fig. 63c). Another new construction was the apron front, sometimes known *(Shoemen's Foreign Terms,* 1921) as the Norwegian or ski (fig. 53), based on the moccasin.

TOES

Although the round and bulldog toes continued into the early 20s (plate 6b), they were out of mood with the new way of life. In c.1918-20 they had been combined with a very short cap, particularly for women, giving a stubby effect. It was the pointed toe which soon predominated (plate 6a), though men's working boots necessarily had a more natural shape. The 22 March 1927 Lotus advertisement in the *Daily Mirror* said: 'short French toes' (pointed). Golding in 1934 remarked that: 'By far the greatest majority of footwear on the market is pointed.'

HEELS

Heels for men remained a standard 1-inch. For women though, according to *Créations Inédites de Paris,* 1925, no. 38: 'the most fashionable heel [the Cuban heel] is from 5 to 5½ cms high' (plate 6a). The louis also continued, with a craze c.1925 for coloured and black lacquer set with pastes (plate 5a). In May 1926 the *Footwear Organiser* told of the: 'Increasing demand of late for novelties of all kinds, especially for jewelled heels . . . for evening and particularly

dancing wear.' From c.1925 there were more slender versions of the louis known from c.1931 as the Spanish heel – *Sunday Graphic* Fashion Contest: 'Navy open saddle tie, Spanish heel.' Both Spanish and Cuban derived from the popularity of Latin-American dances. The early 30s heels were lower, dull, stacked, with half-hearted curves. Golding in 1934 remarked that: 'At the present day very few ladies would consent to wear shoes with heels less than 1½ inches in height'. They were beginning to rise again.

MEN'S

For men, boots continued to predominate. For smart wear, a few buttons continued to c.1930, though the elastic-side went out of fashion soon after 1920. The majority were front lace: bal or Eton-bal and derby,

---

52 *Men's style chart, A.E. Marlow Ltd, Northampton, 1926. Three boots (two open tab). Twelve shoes: 10 oxfords or closed tab, 2 open tab. Note varieties of brogue and the three variations on the two-colour (co-respondent). The golosh oxford is a cut-down bal boot. The cover illustrates a brown oxford with wide lace. The reverse of the chart gives a choice of 14 varieties of perforations for cap edge.*

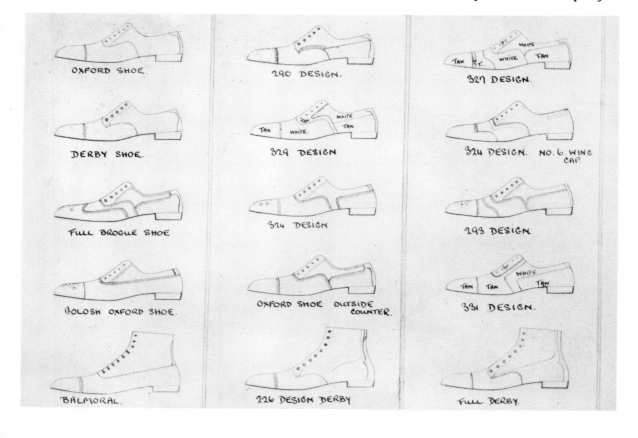

53 *Manfield & Sons Ltd, catalogue, autumn 1927.*
Women's walking and sports shoes: 7 bar shoes (one
with 'light single sole and grey embroidered flowers'
scarcely seems to qualify as a walking shoe). Another
with reptile collar and bar is very typical of its date.
Another has 'crepe rubber golfing sole and heel'.
One court. Two derbys for sports wear (one with
new apron front 'Norwegian cut', and crepe sole).
One brogue oxford. The distribution is typical, the
only other style included in this catalogue being a
high-cut shoe with elasticated gusset front.

the blucher now relegated to working wear, though
there is a photograph of c.1921 of Sir Philip Sassoon
seated in his garden, wearing straight side-seam
bluchers, with a rubber half-sole repair. On 15 January 1921 Kettering *Evening Telegraph* Cash & Co.
boot sale referred to 'dark tan willow Derby 16 shillings 9 pence, glace kid Derby 19 shillings, strong
nailed Derby's 13 shillings 6 pence'.

Shoes also offered a choice of open or closed tab
(fig. 52), derby/Gibson or oxford, now generally
five eyelet. For more decorative wear the Prince of
Wales popularized the brogue shoe with fringed or

Walking & Sports Shoes

No. 271513 . . . . 24/11
In Patent leather, with grey embroidered flowers and stitching. Light single
sole, celluloid covered Louis heel

No. LT429 . 35/-
Sports Shoe, with
buckle, in Brown
Grain Calf. Stout
sole, low heel

No. 27780 . . . . 26/11
Court design in Patent leather, with
light single sole and celluloid covered
Louis heel

No. LT834 . 32/9
Buckle Shoe in
Brown Willow Calf,
with crepe rubber
golfing sole and heel

No. 27703 . . . . 35/-
In Patent leather, with grey watersnake
collar and bar. Light single sole,
celluloid covered Louis heel

No. LT448 . 37/6
Brown Willow
Derby-cut Shoe for
sports wear, with
fawn Lizard strap-
ping. Medium-stout
sole, low heel

Manfield
& SONS LTD

shawl tongue. It is illustrated in the 1921 *Shoe-maker's Foreign Terms*, but was more popular c.1925. Most of the flamboyance was concentrated in the colours and contrasting materials. For evening wear there was still a choice of black patent pumps, or the oxford which was to become *de rigueur*.

WOMEN'S

BOOTS

Women's boots were virtually out for smart wear by 1922, being inappropriate to the new-found freedom and shorter skirts. On 14 August 1920 the *Illustrated London News* advised 'for a chilly summer day or travelling, lace leg boot, high heel, black patent cap' (fig. 57a) and there was still an eighteen-button boot in the United States as late as 1925. Those at Northampton of this date have twenty to twenty-nine pairs of eyelets. They were revived in volume as the Russian, a straight-topped knee-high leather wellington (fig. 57b), with pointed toe and usually a louis heel. In December 1925 the *Footwear Organiser* remarked that: 'The extraordinary demand for Russian boots has spread all over the country. It was first seen in

Walking & Sports Shoes

No. LT434 . 32/9
Norwegian-cut Golf Shoe in Brown Willow Calf, with crepe rubber sole and heel
Also with stout leather sole and heel same price

No. LT831 . . . . 29/9
In Brown Willow Calf, with light welted sole and low heel
Also in Patent, Black Box or Stone Morocco, same price

No. LT452 . 29/9
Light Sports Shoe in Brown Willow Calf, with Crocodile Calf inlets

No. LT436 . . . . 26/11
Strong shoe for country, etc. In Brown Willow Calf, with medium-stout sole and low heel
Same in Box Calf, black, No. LB779, 24/11

No. LT443 . 35/-
Brown Willow Calf Bar design for sports or semi-sports wear, with Stone coloured Calf collar and inlet. Medium welted sole, leather heel

No. LT783 . . . . 26/11
Brogue Shoe in Brown Willow Calf, with stout sole and square heel

Manfield
& SONS Ltd

May 1921 . . a few more each winter.' *The British Shoeman* of May 1921 said that 'The picturesque Russian boots in suede and patent leather caused quite a sensation at the Grand National meeting.' In 1927 'a smarter type of high legged boot, close fitting to the leg' had a zip fastener. The rubber version (fig. 57c) effectively killed the fashion. Thereafter there were only practical rubber wellingtons for wet weather.

SHOES

The predominating style in shoes by 1924 was the single bar fastening with button (plate 5b). On 10 July 1920 the *Illustrated London News* told of the 'four bar, one or two-bar' for summer fashions. The Duchess of York on honeymoon in May 1923 wore a sturdy two-bar shoe. By the 30s, the buckle bar with slide or pronged buckle was more common than a button. There were also cross-bars, particularly with afternoon gowns, and beaded bar shoes for evening (plate 5c). Two-colour combinations were also used from 1921, and became almost as much a trademark of Coco Chanel as her suit. There is a photograph of her in 1929 in beige bar shoe wirh black cap and counter.

There were also T-bars from 1920, usually fastening with buckle, listed as the 'Charleston' in Golding, 1934, though they were more popular in the 30s (plate 5c). In 1933 the girls at the Paramount Astoria dance-hall wore white T-strap sandals with open sides. The lace bar appeared in 1927 in a Lotus advertisement, and became popular in the 30s. Golding, 1934, said that the 'tie shoe is a bar with one or two eyelets.'

The barrette and tango went out of fashion before 1922. The Cromwell style with tab front continued. On 2 January 1922, the *Daily Express* carried a William Whitely Ltd, London, advertisement: 'Cromwell shoes glace kid, handmade, suitable for Dress or Promenade wear . . . usually 36 shillings, sale price 18 shillings.' The buckle was also omitted to create the jester style. In January 1922 the *Daily Express* referred to the ' "Jester" shoe in real glace'. In 1935 *Survey* remarked that 'there has been some harking back to the Jester model and tab courts generally.'

There were some brogue shoes too for women (fig. 51), in a 1922 sale in 'brown and grey, medium toes and heels', or 'pointed toes and Cuban heels; also stamped crocodile calf with fringed tongue, reduced to 15 shillings'. The next year a fringe tab is illustrated in an engraving 'Au Polo', with a high thin heel. The brogue was smart town wear in 1934,

54 Men's brogue oxford shoes, c.1922. (a) Light brown ('yellow') Scotch calf by Pollard, Northampton, 'Guaranteed Hand Made'. Oval toe with winged cap, 1-inch stacked heel. Front lace over tongue, 5 pairs of eyelets. Exhibited at the Shoe & Leather Fair, 1922. (b) One of a pair of blue and beige leather, made by Mounts Factory Co. Ltd, Northampton, probably for exhibition. Pointed toe with blue winged cap, 1-inch stacked brown leather heel. Blue quarters. Front lacing over tongue, 6 pairs of eyelets.

according to Golding. He also says: 'The Derby shoe is not greatly in vogue at present, but it is often produced in very light leathers with modifications such as the Gibson. The latter formerly had three large eyelets, now four or five smaller ones.' All had wide laces. There were also 5-eyelet oxford promenade shoes c.1923. The new tie shoes were ghillies, a traditional Scottish style. Diana Mitford wears a pair in a family portrait of 1929, as does her mother five years later. Golding in 1934 remarked that, 'The ghillie shoe formerly made with seven loops; the present fashion is for five. For golfing and hiking. The laces usually have acorn tags' (fig. 63a).

But four of the shoes in the 1931 Sunday Graphic Fashion Contest were courts (also one ghillie, and seven out of the nine two-colour co-respondent). A photograph of the 'Miss Broadway 1931' New York competition shows all but one in courts, the winner in a co-respondent. The court was the second most popular style, ousting the bar in the 30s (plate 6c). In 1929 W. Bland said: 'Black patent courts were a must for every wardrobe and all seasons.' All the contestants in *The News of the World* Fashion competition of 26 July 1931 wore courts, with asymmetrical trim. The 1933 *Essex County Standard* advertised 'opera court [open side between vamp and quarter] in silver kid, 20 shillings.' The two Northampton-made shoes presented to the Duchess of Kent in 1934 were courts, blue or brown glace. Golding noted in 1934: '. . . originally made for indoor evening wear. Now popular design for everyday wear, indoors and out.'

For wear over the high heels, there were now heelless rubber goloshes, tolerated though never popular for smart wear.

SANDALS

Sandals for summer and beach wear developed in the 30s, beginning with the Sahara sandal, 1931, which in spite of its name seems to have come from Czechoslovakia, based on the moccasin construction: the sole curved up round the edge of the foot and upper was thonged on. The sides between vamp and quarters were generally left open. They became very popular c.1933-5. The year 1931 also saw a fashion which was to develop after 1935: an open toe, open side sandal with sling-back, though open toes became volume fashion before the sling-back.

---

55 Men's boots. (a) One of a pair of bals, brown leather golosh and imitation crocodile leg. Narrow square toe with cap, $1\frac{1}{8}$-inch stacked heel. Front lacing over tongue, 9 pairs of blind eyelets. Back strap; braid loop. Size 6. Early 1920s. (b) One of a pair of black grain derby boots by E. Pollard, Northampton, 25 October 1927. Square toe with cap, 1.1-inch stacked heel. Front lacing over tongue, 8 pairs of eyelets.

△ 56 Men's shoes and sandal. (a) One of a pair of brown leather welted veldtschoens made by Lotus Ltd to their patent 3822/4 of 1914. Round toe, mock cap, 1⅛-inch stacked heel. Front lace over reinforced tongue, 5 pairs of eyelets. Size 8. Guaranteed waterproof. 1930s. (b) Dark brown leather sandal. Footshape toe, 0.6-inch stacked heel. T-strap to buckle over instep. Size 7. 1930s. (c) Light brown Russia calf and white buckskin brogue shoe, made by Manfield, Northampton. Round toe with brown cap and instep strap, 1-inch stacked heel. Front lace over tongue, 6 pairs of blind eyelets. Brown counter. Machine welted. Fully brogued. 1935.

◁ 57 Women's leg boots. (a) Black patent vamp, beige glace kid leg giving gaiter effect, 16 buttons. Narrow oval toe, 2⅝-inch covered heel. Early 1920s. (b) Brown leather Russian boot, made by Joseph Box, London. Pointed toe, 2¾-inch covered louis heel. c.1925. (c) One of a pair of dark brown rubber wellingtons, Delatop by Dunlop. Pointed toe with cap, 1½-inch Cuban heel. Lightning zip. Size 4. c.1927.

8
1935-1952
George VI

Fears about the rise of Hitler and the threat of war with Germany, which began in September 1939 and continued to 1945, formed the basis of this period. There were constitutional problems with the abdication of Edward VIII, replaced by his brother, George VI in 1937, a crisis of confidence for England, all reflected in the aggressive fashions of the time. The immediate postwar years picked up prewar fashions, but with greater austerity, until Dior created the New Look in Paris in 1947. Though Britain could ill afford the extravagant use of material, it was nonetheless adopted. Women's shoes were very slow to adapt, scarcely less clumpy than during the war, which may have suggested that British shoe manufacturers were incapable of designing smart shoes. That this was quite wrong was shown by the men's manufacturers who produced the spiv and Teddy Boy styles for the younger generation.

There were restrictions on the quantity of footwear available during the 40s, clothing being rationed by coupons from 1941 to 1949, seven being required for men's boots and shoes, five for women's. Quality was controlled by the Limitation of Supplies Order, dated September 1941, firms being obliged to produce 50 per cent of shoes to the Utility standard. These were also free of purchase tax. Rubber soles and heels were banned in 1942. In 1948 more shoes were made free of purchase tax. In grade I men's, the highest permitted price was 66 shillings 2 pence, instead of 56 shillings 7 pence; women's 59 shillings 2 pence, instead of 46 shillings 1 penny. Women's clogs during 1942-4 cost two coupons, instead of the five for shoes, but the August 1944 Boot Trades' Association *Gazette* reported: 'The retailer has had great difficulty since just after the inception of wooden soled footwear in persuading his customers to buy this shoe [to relieve the demand for leather]. After the novelty had worn off, retailers began to experience difficulty in maintaining sales.' There still lingered south of the Pennines some association of clogs with poverty and squalid conditions in North Country mills.

There were some technical innovations. *Survey II*, 1935, recorded that: 'Silhouwelt shoes are gaining ground in this country'. The cemented construction was to replace welted and turnshoe for women's light wear. The second change was volume production of the moccasin (figs. 60a, 61c), though not every shoe with apron front had the true moccasin construction. From these too came the casual shoes. The term was first applied to women's, in *Vogue*, June 1950, in advertisements for 'Splendida casuals' — platform sole sling-back, and Holmes' 'Kumfees' casuals, with wedge heels.

MATERIALS
There was a greatly increased use of zips, as Cecil King's Diary, 8 February 1940, recorded on lunch with Winston Churchill: 'Winston wore black boots with zip fasteners, the first I have seen.' A photograph of him in the War Cabinet shows him wearing such boots, with the zip half undone. There were experiments with synthetic materials, plastics from c.1943. They were not very successful and mainly confined to sandals at first. Northampton Museum has some 1943 sandals, with clog sole, and plastic straps reinforced with leather to take the lace. The perspex heels at the end of the period were smarter and worn in some quantity. The May 1950 *Footwear's* Paris Report suggested it was to be a fabric season, using nylon for women's uppers.

But all the comments of the late 30s were on the sheer bulk of footwear. In 1936 it was mentioned: 'The big surprise this autumn will be shoes. They . . . come to the ankle.' That was the year that Ferragamo first made a wedge heel for women's shoes, and by 1938 86 per cent of American shoes had the wedge. The March 1939 *Survey* reported that 'while the platform-sole is a newcomer here, it has a wide public in the United States.' In 1937 even the eyelets were large. *Butterick Fashion Magazine* for winter 1938-9 said: 'Daytime shoes have a bulkier, almost clumsy look . . . wedge heels, platform soles. Afternoon shoes retain some of the bulkiness. . . both built up in front

to give an unbroken line from toe to ankle.' Platform soles were boosted by the film star, Carmen Miranda, 5 feet tall (fig. 64a). In 1939 'Never have shoes been so comfortable'. They were just the thing to cope with a war, and the whole appearance was aggressive – square toes and heels from 1936 (*Shoe and Leather News*, 21 February, reported 'the craze that swept America from coast to coast, a new shoe style with square toes and heels'), and walled uppers in 1941 (plate 7), revived again for men after the war. The average size for women now had risen to 5½, a great contrast to the 2 and 3 of Edwardian times.

COLOURS

There was a surge of colours, particularly during the war. Sherry, or London, tan for both men and women to begin with (figs. 60a, 63c), was followed by wine, maroon (figs. 62b, 63d) and navy or French blue. Besides the old co-respondent colours, many other two-colour combinations were tried, especially the primaries, either in equal quantities (fig. 63d), or as a trim. Colour was good for morale and hid imperfections in the leather, as did the pebble grains which suited the clumpy styles (fig. 61b).

A postwar development in colour was the artificial 'antiquing' of leather, first seen in autumn 1947, which was to develop more in the next period. One of Northampton's wedding gifts to Prince Philip was a pair of gorse calf spectator sports shoes with antique finish.

Of the fashionable materials, there was much suede, and crepe rubber for soling, suitable for bulky shoes. It was also the usual soling for postwar spiv styles, and for the Teds from the 50s on (fig. 59). *Shoe & Leather Record*, 13 April 1950, records: 'Bold Look. The demand for a more spectacular man's shoe is not confined to the young or . . . otherwise loudly-dressed customer. Great demand for crepe-sole wedge heel . . . must be full in the toe. Tan upper able to take antique dressing.' The Teds preferred them with blue suede uppers.

At this time too interweaving began as decoration (fig. 62a), with a Barkers advertisement for 'a man's buckle shoe, interwoven vamp', 6 July 1950. The September *Footwear* carried the note: 'Dolcis, the new slotted theme,' and in April 1951 George Webb's 'Mexican laced step-ins, with interlaced apron.' It developed in the early 60s as an upper fabric with Italian imports.

◁ 58 *'Conversation Piece, Royal Lodge, Windsor', by James Gunn, in oil, 1950. It shows the King in brown oxford shoes, his wife in red courts, and the two princesses in brown sling-back court shoes.*

---

59 *'British Quality', no.4, Shoe & Leather Record, 1951. Three men's shoes from British Bata with thick crepe soles in the 'spiv' style: one with traditional brogue oxford upper, the other two-colour, with saddle effect, a 1940s style; left with white apron, 2 straps to buckle; bottom right 4-eyelet tie.*
▽

TOES

Toes for both sexes were deep round or footshape, with some square walled toes during the War (as fig. 62b). There were more peep toes after 1935, and the open toe on sandals was accepted (fig. 64a). Mrs Simpson wore them at Cannes in a photograph with the Prince of Wales, though other women in the picture wear strap sandals or courts. The 1947 New Look required a more elegant shoe, and in Paris Dior showed it with what *Vogue* described in April as 'pointed Spanish pumps'. But Britain had still not accepted them in May 1950. *Footwear* recorded

'The square toe versus the slender pointed toe is the basis of much discussion.' The most extreme could only be described as a very blunt point.

HEELS

Ferragamo's 1936 wedge heel had proved ideal for wartime economy, which leather substitutes such as cork becoming popular, and customers rarely discovering what was under the leather cover. They were carved into sculptured shapes (fig. 64b & c), encouraging makers to experiment with other heels: a lobed heel on a Bally shoe of 1946, square top pieces the same year (fig. 65b) and the Brevitt Bouncers etc. with internal heel, 1948 (fig. 65d). In 1949, on 23 June, *Shoe & Leather Record* announced: 'London acclaims wedges for men. They are not new, John Winter & Son Ltd. have been making them for the past three years.' There were also smart low-heeled shoes for women, said to have been pioneered by Miss McCardell in the United States in 1944, or with platform and sling-back, for casual wear. But the 1949 December *Footwear* recorded 'royal patronage of the platform and ankle straps has fostered a public

60 Men's shoes. (a) One of a pair of tan leather slip-on casual shoes (the contemporary term was 'slipper') by Lotus Ltd, Northampton. Round toe, ¾-inch stacked heel. Instep strap stitched over apron front. The 'Norwegian moccasin' (apron front) was new in 1936. (b) Light brown suede 'monk tie' (the contemporary description) by Crockett & Jones, Northampton. Round toe, 1-inch stacked heel. Two pairs of eyelets. A rather daring fashion at this date. c.1943.

5 Women's court, bar and T-bar shoes. (a) One of a pair of evening courts, of silver, mauves and greens brocade by Pinet, Paris. Blunt pointed toe, $2\frac{7}{8}$-inch 'jewelled' heel set with pastes and enamel. c.1925. (b) Red satin bar shoe with red sequins, black and white bead embroidery, made in France for Harrods Ltd. Pointed toe, 2.6-inch embroidered louis heel. Bar to button over instep. White kid quarter lining and sock. c.1925. (c) One of a pair of black satin T-bar shoes from Gardos, Vienna. Pointed toe, 2½-inch covered louis heel. Paste embroidery. c.1926.

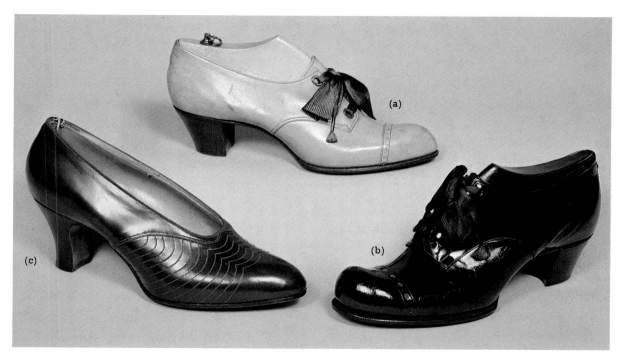

6 Women's Gibson and court shoes. (a) One of a pair of light tan glace kid Gibsons, made by Crockett & Jones, Northampton. Pointed toe with cap, brogued edge, 2-inch stacked Cuban heel. Front lace over peaked tongue, 3 pairs of oval eyelets, wide brown silky lace. Green suede lining. 1922. (b) One of a pair of black patent Gibsons, made by Crockett & Jones. Bulldog toe with cap, brogued edge, 1½-inch stacked Cuban heel. Black finish under arch. Front lace over tongue, 5 pairs of blind eyelets, wide silky lace. 1923. (c) Navy blue kid court. Health brand by Crockett & Jones. Blunt pointed toe, $2\frac{5}{8}$-inch covered louis heel. Cemented sole; decorative vamp stitching. Size 4. c.1933.

Sexton Son & Everard

NORWICH

AGENTS :

NEW ZEALAND
Messrs. H. M. Marler & Co., Ltd.
Ellison Chambers, Queen Street
Auckland

BARBADOES, B.W.I.
Mr. J. H. Haigh
P.O. Box 128
Bridgetown

SOUTH AFRICA
Mr. A. C. DePinna
P.O. Box 6732
Johannesburg

7 'Leadership of British Footwear', in *Footwear Organiser*, December 1940. Sexton, Son & Everard advertisement. The colours are typical of this period. From top to bottom: the brown snakeskin and suede Oxfordette is typical of the late 1930s, but has the walled toe of the 1940s. Comfortable red suede tie shoe with crepe sole, a smart walking shoe. Two-colour wedge heeled shoe. Note perforated vamp. Tie shoe with tab to conceal lacing, platform sole.

61　Men's clog and Demobilization shoes. (a) One of
a pair of brown leather derby clogs, made by Long
Buckby Shoes Ltd. Round toe, $1\frac{3}{8}$-inch heel with
leather top piece. Wooden sole has leather strips to
cut down noise, which most of England was not used
to. Punching to accentuate the smooth leather saddle.
c.1943. (b) One of a pair of brown grain leather
oxfords, made by Allinson & Co., Northampton. One
of the styles issued to demobilized servicemen in
1945. Round toe with cap, 1-inch stacked heel,
5 pairs of eyelets. (c) One of a pair of brown leather
derby shoes made by Norvic Ltd, Northampton. One
of the styles issued to demobilized servicemen in
1945. Square toe, $1\frac{1}{8}$-inch heel, rubber top piece.
Rubber sole. Apron front, 5 pairs of eyelets.

62　Men's crepe sole shoes. (a) One of a pair of
brown leather strap shoes. Round toe, 1.2-inch heel.
Strap to buckle over instep. Interlacing on vamp.
Northampton College of Technology final year student work, 1951. (b) Maroon leather lace shoe.
Round walled toe, 1½-inch wedge heel. Sole $\frac{5}{8}$-inch
thick at front. Apron front, open tab, D-rings to lace.
Interwoven brown thong. Teddy Boy wear, early
1950s.

△

63 Women's shoes and clog. (a) One of a pair of brown suede and glace oxfordette shoes by K Shoes, Kendall, 'as illustrated in Vogue', price 20 shillings. Oval toe with glace cap, $3\frac{3}{8}$-inch covered louis heel. Glace quarters. Front lace over tongue, 4 pairs of blind eyelets, white striped tags. The high cut, lines of stitching and punching are typical. c.1935.
(b) Navy blue suede ghillie tie by Crockett & Jones, Northampton. Broad round toe, 1¼-inch heel. Natural crepe rubber sole. Crimson welt stitched in white.

Pale blue leather piping. c.1940. (c) One of a pair of sherry tan leather shoes by H.E. Randall Ltd, Northampton. Square toe, 1.9-inch stacked Cuban heel. Elastic gusset under stitched-down tab. 1940. (d) One of a pair of maroon suede and blue leather clogs, by True-Form Ltd, Northampton. Round toe, 1½-inch heel, leather top piece. 0.4-inch wooden sole with leather patches to cut down noise. Open tab, front lace, 4 pairs of eyelets. Leather saddle. c.1943.

demand' (fig. 58). The new platforms were shallow, and toe shapes moderate (fig. 65c). The straight Cuban tended to overshadow the louis, which survived mainly in the slim Spanish heel.

Platform soles had naturally gone with wedge heels, though regarded as rather fast until Princess Elizabeth, wishing to add a little to her height at her wedding in 1947, wore a pair. They were somewhat tentatively tried by men, but never became popular except in crepe (fig. 59), averaging about ½ inch. In 1952 a man's casual shoe was made unlined, with microcellular rubber sole, though this was to develop later.

MEN'S

For men, shoes predominated over boots by 1935, except for labouring work, brown increasing at the expense of black. There was still the choice of oxford or derby, though no Victorian would have recognized the decorated post-war styles. A new style was the monk, with narrower latchets taking either the buckle and strap, or two pairs of eyelets (fig. 60b). Another was the casual moccasin (fig. 60a). Two of the seven 1945 demobilization shoes had apron fronts with open tab — one black, one brown (fig. 61c). The rest had toe caps. All seven had five pairs of eyelets, three in black, three brown leather and one brown suede; three oxfords (fig. 61b), two derbies. This gives a useful indication of the plain popular styles. The 1947 collection presented by Northampton bootmakers to Prince Philip shows a livelier range. Besides the spectator sports, it included 'tan full brogue, lightweight, wholecut tie veldtschoen, two-colour apron front golf shoe, willow calf oxford and a suede monk shoe with crepe sole.' Brogues were especially

popular (fig. 59). The male was obviously craving for more decoration. John Winter, who pioneered wedges, offered in 1949 brogues, half-brogues, plain oxford or derby, and fancy oxfords.

SANDALS

Sandals for summer wear began to develop too. A photograph of the Men's Dress Reform Party in 1937 shows one in a T-strap sandal (fig. 56b), one in a two-colour tie, and four plain ties. Reform had scarcely reached the feet. By the early 50s sandals were losing the arty image and becoming acceptable for all. Northampton Museum has a crepe-soled sandal with wide vamp straps and sling-back to buckle.

WOMEN'S

For women too there were few boots: mainly utilitarian sheepskin, ankle high, for winter. Frequently of suede and front lace at first (Randall made a pair of brown leather in 1939, with apron front, front lace, seven pairs of eyelets), they adopted the zip after the war. In 1949 John Winter at Simpsons was charging for 'wine, blue or black suede 124 shillings or tan calf 127 shillings, crepe wedge, zip.' One of the 1947 wedding presents to Princess Elizabeth from Northampton bootmakers was a pair of lamb-lined bootees with crepe sole. A few smarter ankle boots were made. Northampton Museum has a turquoise glace pair with paisley cuff, c.1935, but they never became volume fashion.

The lace shoes at first were high-cut oxfordettes (plate 7 & fig. 63a), with higher heels, and decorated with rows of stitching and punching in jazzy angular designs. The lower heeled walking shoes were gibsons with saddle (as fig. 63d), which appeared as early as the 1936 Boot Manufacturers' Federation Year Book. A 1948 pair by Manfield, black leather, four pairs of eyelets cost 55 shillings 10 pence. There were a considerable number too of spectator sports shoes worn with tweed suits, with 1½-inch Cuban heel, a practical compromise during rationing.

The dress shoe of the 30s was the plain court with medium heel. But these were soon modified with asymmetrical trims, peep toes and sling-back. Jean Harlow wore a co-respondent in 1932 with mock sling-back appliqué. In 1936 a pair of Bally blue suede courts for a wedding cost one guinea and had a 3¾-inch louis heel. (Mrs Patricia Nixon wore at her wedding in 1940 a court with a side dip.) Lana Turner wore a white high cut perforated shoe with sling-back in 1937. The Shoe & Leather Record, of 16 June 1949 says: 'As it has been the accepted rule

◁ 64 *Women's sandals, 1936-40. (a) One of a pair of morning or beach clogs by R.R. Bunting, London & Paris. Footshape toe, 4-inch heel. Wooden sole. 1-inch high at front. Grey tweed toe-band and T-strap to buckle. Leather insole acts as hinge to segmented wooden sole. (b) One of a pair of black suede sandals by Lotus Ltd, 'hand fashioned'. Round peep toe, 3-inch covered wedge heel cut out and lined with red kid. Sling-back to buckle round ankle. Red sock edge and stitching. Late 1930s. (c) One of a pair of black suede sandals with green, blue and red suede and gold kid, from Harrods Ltd. Pointed toe, 3½-inch covered triple wedge heel (popular in 1941). Black and gold sling-back to fasten with diamanté buckle. Peach satin sock. Late 1930s.*

that this country should follow Paris in fashions, it was something of an occasion to hear . . . that women in Paris . . . are wearing sling-backs and peep-toes. Women in Britain have all along demanded these features in their summer shoes, despite the onrush of new "closed-in" looks.' France was beginning to lose its fashion lead (fig. 65b). There were ankle straps too from 1936, though not in volume until 1942, and more respectable in 1947 (fig. 65c). Most of Dior's mannequins the next year had ankle-strap courts or open sandals. The plain court was modified too in the late 40s. The *Shoe & Leather Record* for 7 July 1949 said: 'Some of the smartest courts are undoubtedly those with square cut foreparts . . . . Foot-gloves court with fancy stitched upper 59 shillings.' The early 50s brought shocking pinks and pale greens, and the Jester court.

Other high cut shoes included slip-ons with a tab over an elastic front (fig. 63c), which was most popular during the war, and again worn with the suit.

As well as the ankle strap, there were a few with instep strap, the old bar style, but far different from the 20s. They began as an American style and came over as California imports under the Joyce label, in c.1947 in red leather with wide bar, platform sole and wedge heel, and in 1950 Brevitt Bounder with instep strap to buckle.

SANDALS

Near nudity on the foot became acceptable during this period, to suit the craze for sunbathing (fig. 64a).

There were open toes; open sides by 1937, and cut-outs all over the vamp the same year. A Seeberger photograph of Biarritz in 1938 shows white platform sole sandals with apron front. For a brief period in c.1943 there were clog soles, and cork and raffia were used for smart sandals during the War to release leather for more important purposes, many of the French austerity sandals looking highly desirable. In 1946 straw sandals with a platform sole unit were imported from Italy, a foretaste of problems to come. By the early 50s sandals consisting of a few thin straps had arrived.

---

65 *Women's shoes, 1945-8. (a) One of a pair of black suede and grey lizard court shoes. Round toe, lizard cap, 2¾-inch covered narrow wedge heel. Lizard quarters; pink lining and sock. c.1945. (b) One of a pair of navy blue cloth and calf sling-back courts by Brevitt Ltd, bought April 1947 for £3.7.6 (expensive), the first high-heeled shoes available after the war. Round peep toe, 3.4-inch calf covered heel, square top piece. Calf sling-back to buckle, with elastic inside. Calf binding and rosette. (c) One of a pair of black leather and imitation crocodile ankle strap shoes. Round toe, 3-inch crocodile covered heel; ¼-inch crocodile platform sole. Strap to buckle round ankle. Utility mark inside. (d) One of a pair of black leather casual shoes, Saskatoon style from Dolcis. Round toe, wedge heel covered by quarters. Elasticated top edge. Maroon piping and bow. c.1948.*

9
1953-
Elizabeth II

1953 was coronation year, the new Elizabethan age. Changes indeed there were, with the end of austerity and an affluence which spread to all levels of society to an extent never seen before. By 1964 when the Labour government was elected, some said that power was in the hands of the unions and the workers. Labour remained in office with one interval to 1979. The first part of the period exhibited a succession of styles still based on Paris designs, with the desire to dress as ladies and gentlemen. But the baby boom of the 1940s produced a strong sub-culture of teenage youth, with its own personality, expressed particularly in pop music. By the early 60s, with the rise of The Beatles, this was percolating through to older generations. The adoption by both sexes of jeans, originally American working men's wear, and the attendant scruffiness, typified the glorification of the working man, and woman's hope for equality. By the late 70s, there were signs of change again, the jeans no longer faded and patched, and women began to look like ladies again in pretty flowery dresses, a change back to conservatism, which was how the country voted in 1979. Anything (almost) now goes, from shabby jeans, repulsive punk, to expensive elegance, signs of the deep divisions within society.

Since 1960 people have expressed themselves through dress more than at any other time, with no set fashion for all. The variety, linked with sub-cultures and political changes, suggests how much more might be gleaned from the past by more intensive study. When Piccadilly rose in indignation at Lord Randolph's brown boots, it was not because brown boots are in themselves offensive, though I am not sure about safety pins through noses: in both cases it is the threat of non-conformity they represent. Dress should not be taken lightly.

COLOUR AND MATERIALS
With the explosion of affluence and sheer energy of youth, there was an enormous choice of colours: beige, pearlized pastels (fig. 72a), and orange in 1957-9. A True-Form tangerine court with stiletto heel 49

shillings 11 pence was reduced to 29 shillings in a 1960 summer sale. Chanel re-launched the co-respondent (fig. 72c), with consequences (fig. 74a). Even the conventional browns were 'antiqued' (figs. 67, 69c). In the early 70s the extremes were reached with bright primaries, silver and gold combined with outrageous platforms. Colours have noticeably subdued with the recession.

There were developments of new materials, especially attempts to give plastic the breathability of leather. Corfam (a poromeric) was developed by DuPont, USA, 1963, and used first by Rayne for women's courts, and tried out at Northampton College of Technology in 1964. It was used for cheaper shoes in the United States that year, though prices were kept high in Britain. Cheaper plastics were also tried for uppers. The *Sunday Times* of 1 September 1963 reported: 'The latest synthetic leather, hot on the heels of St Laurent who showed boots in the real thing, is mock croc, from Lotus 3 gns.' It was used for both men's and women's (fig. 69a). In 1956 the first injection-moulded sandals were made in Britain, similar to fig. 70a. There were women's plastic evening shoes by 1958 (fig. 72b) and Rayne advertised on 12 April 1966 in the *Sunday Times* 'Transparent PVC sling-backs 12 guineas.' Tanners competed with wet-look leather, indistinguishable at a distance from plastic.

To cope with rising prices, more shoes were made unlined, *Shoe & Leather Record* of 10 September 1959: 'Unlined suede gibsons' and in 1961 Reveille commented: 'Some shoes are now made of leather which before the War might have been used for gloves. Women want soft light shoes.'

There was competition too from a new leather, brushed pigskin, hitherto little used for shoes. Patented in the United States in 1957, it was imported and made under licence under the name Hush Puppies (fig. 73c). Used at first only for low-heeled lace shoes, the only comfortable shoe in the winkle-picker period, it graduated to casuals and courts, as a more casual style of dressing was accepted in the 60s. It

66 *Women's shoes,* Vogue, *September 1959. Note that nos. 1 and 3 are square at the toe.*

This season's pump shows the long, lean grace of a wolfhound, its toe drawn out to a thin line that is flat as a pancake when seen in profile. Its height is the result of a sometimes skinny, sometimes waisted heel.

1. Dark brown calf with an underslung heel, lightly squared toe, tabbed vamp. Pancaldi, 5 gns., Mondaine, Bond St., Knightsbridge.

2. Tan calf based on a widely scooped heel, tie-throated. By Airborne, 59s. 11d. at A. Jones, Brompton Road.

3. Tan shrunk-calf, squared at the toe; the diagonal side stitching ending in two pearl buttons. By C. & J. Clark, 49s. 11d. at D.H. Evans

4. Dark grey kid, fine-heeled pump with a shallow cross decorating the vamp. £4. 9s. 11d., Dolcis West End branches

FOR OTHER SHOPS AT WHICH TO BUY THE SHOES: SEE PAGE 265

Toes: elongated, levelled to a flat, wafer-thin line

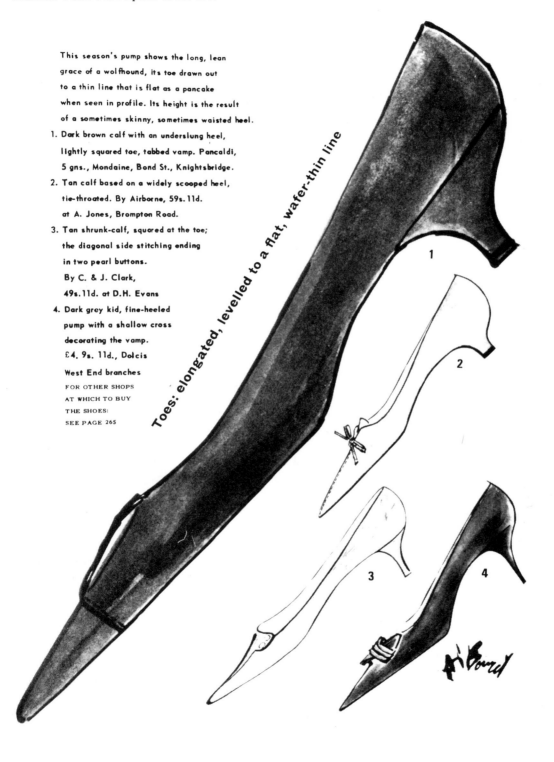

67 Freeman's Mail Order, autumn & winter catalogue, 1963. Men' shoes: the first four are black, the
last two brown. Note 'Italian inspired'. C and G

chisel toe. F also chisel toe, 'antique finished'. All are
smart, younger men's wear. A and C also acceptable
for older executives.

A B8601 The modern tapered toe is displayed in
this Italian inspired black box calf Oxford shoe with
decorative hand stitching on toes and sides, resin
rubber soles and shaped heels.
5 to 11 in ½ sizes 57/6

B B8626 Dashing high-front casual in black fully
chromed leather, with crocodile pattern fronts and
button effect, elastic side gussets, long tapered toes,
resin soles.
6 to 11 in ½ sizes 55/9

C B8629 Be up-to-date and completely "with it" in
these elegantly styled black leather Chelsea boots
with smart chisel toe shape, elastic side gussets, rubber
top-piece heels.
5 to 11 in ½ sizes 62/9

D B8597 A popular, smart and up-to-date Italian-
styled shoe in black full chrome leather with the
latest almond toe shape and side lacing, durable
resin rubber soles and shaped heels.
5 to 11 in ½ sizes 59/6

F B8599 Stylish brass hooks give an added interest
to these side-laced shoes of antique finished whisky-
brown leather, with the new double diamond toe-
shape, resin rubber soles.
5 to 11 in ½ sizes 56/9

G B8596 Sleek and debonair—antiqued mahogany
leather shoes, with long fronts, and chiselled toe line,
resin soles.
6 to 11 in ½ sizes 56/9

was off-duty wear for the 1964 men's British Olympic team, in a side-gusset style. By 1965 Rayne was advertising napped as well as shining Corfam, and in 1972 began the blue suede shoe revival for Teddy Boys, supposedly extinct since 1958.

There were fabric shoes too, such as corduroy in 1964 (fig. 70c) and blue canvas, especially in the early 60s (fig. 70b is an early example) to go with jeans. Sportswear was adopted for daily use to the end of the period. *The Times* of 3 September 1966 referred to 'American youngsters in frayed worn look tennis shoes.' Bowling shoes were worn for disco dancing from 1964. In April 1965 *Nova* advertised Mr Sneekers: 'A familiar character in three continents, but new to Britain.' In 1969 a blue denim crepe sole casual from Topper shoes cost 59 shillings 11 pence, blue canvas boots from Sids 7 guineas. In 1972 'Joe di Maggio baseball boot in blue and yellow leather £14.25.' In 1975 blue and white Adidas sneakers cost £9 45 pence. In 1970-71 knee-high canvas boots were worn by smart women (fig. 74b), though summer clogs in canvas survived longer (fig. 74c).

Plastic soles for women were beginning to replace leather in 1958. In 1967 99.5 per cent were non-leather, and leather-soled footwear in general constituted only 9 per cent. Rubber was accepted for soling. The CEMA process for attaching soles, patented in 1932 by Mediano of Barcelona, was developed in England in 1949 and especially from 1955, when Britton's began to make Tuf boots for men. In 1961 army boots changed to the direct moulded sole (rubber), and in 1967 Dr Marten's patent for plastic cushion soles was exploited. Manufacturers were at last beginning to rethink shoe making, using the new materials, including injection-moulded plastic shoes. Neither attractive nor comfortable, they were tried for golf and beach, but abandoned for general wear, except in the Third World.

The new reign at last brought the sharply pointed toe. On 24 September 1953 the *Shoe & Leather Record* called them 'pointed Spanish toes'; the 1958 *Buyers' Register*, 'needle toe', but they were eventually designated winkle-picker. In 1960 the British Shoe Corporation attempted to introduce a square toe, and the next year there was talk of a fingertip and squared-off toe from Charles Jourdan, Paris. The winkle-picker was ceremonially buried at the Shoe Fair in January. By October the few squares were on men's shoes. But on 16 April 1962 the *Daily Telegraph* reported 'victory for the winkle-picker. Britain's shoemakers have abandoned the square toe. They have declared independence from the influence of the great French designers . . . . In some shops in Britain it never went out.' It was christened 'the square toe debacle', and Manfield's admitted that 'the square never really caught on with our customers.' At the Harrogate spring shoe show in 1964 it

68 *Elton John photographed for the* Daily Mirror, *22 March 1973. Walking tall, pop singer Elton John in his remarkable platform sole boots. He had his boots made to measure, giving him an extra 6 inches in height.*

was reported 'a figure in trousers with a Merseyside hairstyle and pointed-toed footwear, with shaped heels, can be of either sex.' But that year there were more oval and square toes. Britain was now ready for the change. In January 1965 'Jourdan and Vivier all plump for . . . broad toes.' On 25 February 1968 *The Observer* noted that 'toes are rounder than ever'. On 1 March 1970 it said: 'A lot of shoes have become downright ugly and it is high time they were fined down again . . . away from the orthopaedic look.' From 1975 there were hints of the winkle-picker returning, and they began to be popular in 1978. The *Northampton Chronicle & Echo* said on 6 October: 'Pinched toes . . . court shoes for women: We have been selling them like hot cakes for the last four or five months. Also pinched toes for men . . . . If you're punk, they say, you'll go for the new wave of winkle-pickers.' Comfortable round toes are still available.

HEELS

The complement to the pointed toe of the 50s for women was the stiletto heel, first mentioned in the *Daily Telegraph* on 10 September 1953. In 1955 'the trend in Italy is for higher and thinner heels. The exaggeratedly slender heel is not so sought after in

this country, because it breaks so easily.' The problem was solved with a metal spigot and moulded plastic heels which played havoc with floors, and stilettos were banned from many public buildings (figs. 72a & b). Delman of New York, in 1958, had some particularly vicious toes and heels in red patent, shocking pink, as well as black. In 1959 Vivier introduced a comma heel, which looked even more likely to break, and in 1960 there were some shoes cantilevered as for a high heel, with no heel at all. *The*

---

69 *Men's winkle-picker shoes and Beatle boot.*
(a) One of a pair of grey pearlized imitation crocodile and black calf buckle shoes. Winkle-picker toe, 1½-inch stacked heel. Plastic sole. High black tongue with strap buckling at side. Sock stamped: 'Styled in Italy by Ideal Shoemakers' (Kettering). Size 7. 1960. (b) Black leather Beatle boot. Very narrow square toe, 2⅝-inch plastic heel. Elastic gusset each side. Braid loops to pull on. Sock stamped :'Lugano's, Italy'. Size 8. c.1964. (c) One of a pair of side-lace shoes of antiqued brown leather. Winkle-picker toe, 1½-inch stacked heel, plastic top piece and sole. High cut, mock apron. Sock stamped: 'Benevento'. Size 9. c.1965.

Daily Telegraph asked in September 'will the louis heel oust the stiletto?' but in October 1961 'Even though the square toe has virtually laid down and died, the stiletto refuses to do so.' In 1962 it reported: 'Heels . . . you wear them as high or as low as suits you . . . the actual base is a little wider than the stiletto.' But it was not until January 1963 that the *Sunday Times* reported from Florence: 'Not one stiletto heel pierced the catwalk. Instead, Varese's sturdily heeled, sensibly laced ankle ties in printed silk . . . look like plimsolls fished from a dye pot . . . they stump along like surgical boots.' And in March 1964, election year, 'the lower heels which have been on the way for so long are well and truly here. There certainly isn't a stiletto in sight for day.' In 1968 heels rose again to complement the midi skirt, and in 1970 they were changing shape again: straighter, as opposed to the lavatory pan effect of the early midi shoes. By 1970 there were wedges. In January 1971 there were 'monster boats with vast club-like wedges, weighty legacies from the hideous Victoriana of Lancashire Mills.' The alternative was a high, straight heel combined with platform sole, as aggressive and clumsy as the toes. In July 1973 *The Observer* reported: 'Down Kensington High Street I saw a girl teetering on stiletto heels and platform soles. Crazy!' By November Zapata had launched the needle heel: 'absolutely nothing to do with nostalgia', it said, but looking just like a stiletto. There were a few more in 1975, but like the winkle-picker, were not to become volume fashion until 1979-80. In March 1979 Russell

& Bromley advertised an early 50s style court at £27 99 pence, and the British Shoe Corporation promoted a suede court with cone heel in autumn 1979 at £17 99 pence. The wedges continued, becoming especially popular from 1975.

Men fortunately never wore the stiletto, though there was a higher heel in the 60s. In 1961 The Beatles pop group began wearing cowboy boots (figs. 71a, 69b) and the younger generation followed, the first time high heels for men had been popular since the 1720s. Most settled for about 1½ inches. By 1975 they had joined women in wearing wedges, and in 1976 returned to high-heeled cowboy boots, this time in tans and browns, with Texas-style stitching.

---

70 Men's sandal and boots. (a) PVC plastic sandal. Round toe, '1-lift' heel. Four straps, T and sling-back to buckle, all riveted to sole. 'Sarraizienne, Qualité France'. Worn in the south of France, August 1956. (b) Sneaker boot of white-flecked blue canvas, with yellow lace. Round toe, rubber mudguard, no heel. Rubber sole with black and yellow edging. Front lace over tongue, 6 pairs of large eyelets. Cuff with studs. Younger generation wear from Steve Clarke & Sons, Northampton. c.1965-6. (c) One of a pair of brown corduroy boots. Tapered square toe, 1-inch heel. Crepe rubber sole and heel unit, veldtschoen, white stitched. Open tab, front lace, 2 pairs of eyelets, black lace. Brown leather lining. Size 41. Made and bought in Italy, 1964.

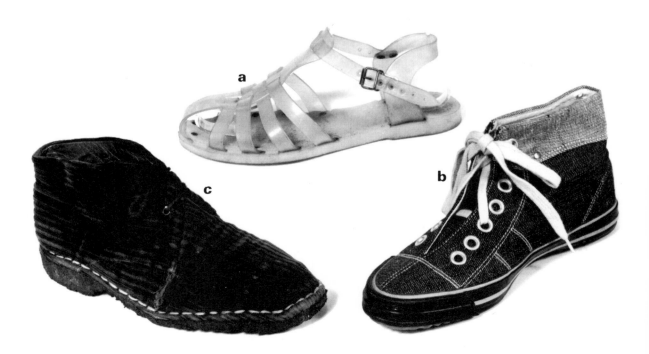

'First made an impression on London fashions two or three years ago' (*Chronicle & Echo*, 30 July 1976). In 1975 Earth shoes with negative heels came from their inventor, Anne Kalso of Copenhagen via the United States where the Roots brand had been a sensation in 1975-6, and a number were tried out the next year, but found to be as uncomfortable as the high heel. But they suited the 'back to nature' trend.

The most outrageous fashion of this period was the platform sole, a revival of the 40s style, but taken to greater heights, though not as high as the sixteenth century chopines. Paloma Picasso claimed to have designed the first one in 1968, though Vivier had made an open toe, ankle-strap sandal with platform in January 1967, in black and white Corfam. At first they were only worn by women. In 1969 a red cross-strap sandal with ½-inch platform by Chelsea Cobbler cost 12 guineas. By 1971 they were attached to 'astonishing boots with shocking pink platform soles' (about 2 inches), and to sandals (fig. 74c). *The Sun* of 3 August 1972 said that 'Clogs were clobbered by medical and fashion experts. Each of these shoes weighs one pound.' By now the men had to follow suit or be literally looked down on (figs. 68 & 71c). They had disappeared by 1978.

MEN'S

SHOES

For men lace-up shoes continued from the previous period, especially the more adjustable gibson, now reduced to two pairs of eyelets, and in browns rather than black, with antiquing, moc-croc and interlacing for decoration. By 1960 there were interwoven leather uppers which the Italians had been wearing

---

71 Men's boot and shoes. (a) 'Cowboy' boot of black leather with white plastic star, made by G.T. Hawkins Ltd, Northampton, 1967; the same style had previously been exported to Texas. Narrow rounded toe, 1½-inch stacked heel. V-dip at front. Yellow stitching. Leather straps inside to pull on. Size 8.
(b) Black leather loafer, made by Clarke & Co, Rushden. Square toe, 1.45-inch fawn stacked heel. Fawn 'real leather' sole. Apron front with mock lace and tassels, collar and outside counter. Size 8½. c.1970.
(c) One of a pair of black leather and rubber platform sole shoes. Square toe with cap, 1½-inch rubber sole rising to 2.4-inch at heel. Front lace over tongue, 3 pairs of eyelets. Outside counter. Plastic lined. Trade mark on sock: 'S' beneath a crown. c.1976.

for comfort in summer. There were also casual slip-on shoes, frequently with apron front, derived from the 30s 'slipper' (fig. 60a), via the United States. Raymond Chandler's *Playback*, 1958, described one of the characters: 'He was California from the tips of his port-wine loafers to the buttoned and tieless brown and yellow check shirt' — though the name 'loafers' was unfamiliar in Britain as yet. By 1967 there was frequently a gilt chain trim across the apron, which was to become an important feature for most men. 'Moccasins' were volume fashion by 1969, though the tassels became more popular from 1972 and in the late 70s, described in 1979 as 'Upmarket loafers'.

BOOTS

From the late 50s there were elastic side boots claiming to be copies of the Edwardian Chelsea, for smart wear. In September 1960 'new versions of the chukka and Chelsea boot . . . give that long lean shoe look that goes with the latest types of trousers', and Harrods advertised the next year 'Chelsea boot, sprung sides . . . styled for the tapered trouser.' The Beatles added a higher heel and the young soon copied them, with zip boots for the staider generation following. There was even an attempt to introduce them for evening wear with trousers tucked in, but the longer legs were resisted until the brown cowboy boots worn with jeans c.1975.

WOMEN'S

SHOES

The principal shoe for women of the 50s to early 60s was the court, usually with trim (fig. 72a), getting more fussy after 1957, occasionally with instep strap from 1961, and the next year: 'the sling-back has the flavour . . . of spring, 1962' (fig. 72c). There were hints of change at this time, and the lower-heeled trotteurs with brass trim, horseshoes etc. were a relief after the high stiletto. On 12 June 1966 the *Sunday Times* mentioned 'status symbol accessories: Gucci shoes, miniature gilt stirrups £8 50 pence per pair'. The Saxone copy sold at 89 shillings 11 pence and an American version the same year at £3. Though some clung to their status symbols, they were less popular after 1970. In 1962-3 some very low heeled shoes, still with needlepoint toe, were imported from Italy (fig. 73b), though most preferred Hush Puppies. By the late 60s they too had higher heels and were treated like other shoes. In 1968 *The Observer* remarked that 'Sensible shoes and fashionable shoes no longer mean two different things' — though with the development of the platform, women soon had to learn to walk all over again.

72 Women's shoes and mule. (a) Pearlized green leather court. Needlepoint toe, 3¾-inch covered stiletto heel. Cut-outs on vamp. Size 4. Lady Orchid style from Newbold & Burton, 1956. (b) Clear plastic mule. Needlepoint toe, 3¾-inch metallic cloth covered stiletto heel. 'Spring-o-lator' elastic grip in sole. Multi-colour plastic leaves and bell decoration. Marsha style from Delman, New York, 1958. (c) One of a pair of black kid and white buckskin sling-back shoes. Blunt pointed toe, 2-inch covered heel, squared off. Size 2. Made by Massaro, Paris, designed and worn by Coco Chanel, based on her 1920s design, re-launched in the 50s. Early 1960s.

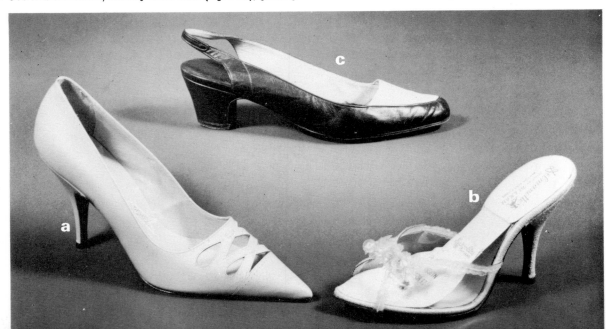

By 1975 the 30s oxfordette styles were beginning to be revived, though more widely adopted in 1979-80. Moccasins and loafers continued. By 1980 the main choices were court, oxford or loafer. 'Loafers have come into their own with the advent of baggy jeans, now for both sexes', it was said on 24 February 1980.

BOOTS

But the change which did take off in 1960 was fashion boots. On 4 September *The Observer* noted: 'There is something of a boom developing in leather knee boots for both girls and boys. Boots for beatniks cost anything between 8 and 10 guineas. The craze for girls' boots was encouraged by Brigitte Bardot. With very high heels, makes girls feel bigger and rather more confident.' In 1961 there were also 'ankle boots [Victorian inspired] to wear with slacks or jeans'. The Americans had worn a smart ankle-high version. The secretary, Miss Vermilyea, in Chandler's *Playback* 1958, wore a 'white-belted raincoat . . . bootees to match.' Boots were a must for everyone by September 1962 (fig. 73a). In 1963 they went thigh high, for the brave, 'neither a fetish nor waterproof', according to the Manufacturers' Federation. In 1966 it was space boots; in 1967 'the kind of boots . . . once worn only by Principal Boys, Guardsman style by Ravel 14 guineas', and by 1969 they were vaguely cavalier, with large buckles on the instep. The lower ankle boot had become the trouser

shoe by 1965, and by 1969 'is fast replacing the boot as the in-thing to wear with trousers for spring.' 'Trousers', *New Society* said in 1970, 'encourage women to wear shoes of an almost male level of comfort, because footsize shoes don't look so enormous.' Many schoolgirls were now taking size 7 or 8, as women grew taller. In 1975 they were wearing cowboy boots like the men, but reverted to the ankle

---

73 *Women's boot, shoes and clog. (a) Black and white plastic boot, with white stripes. Square toe, 1.3-inch heel. White sole and heel unit. Calf-high, zip up inside. Red felt lining with label: 'Souillac, Bordeaux'. Courrèges style. Early 1960s. (b) Red leather shoe with black patent straps. Needlepoint toe, ½-inch wedged heel. Low cut upper, open sides. Sock stamped: 'Parmen, Italy'. Size 36. c.1962-3. (c) Greenish brushed pigskin (by Wolverine, USA) lace shoe. Blunt pointed toe, $\frac{7}{8}$-inch rubber heel with sole unit. Open tab, front lace over tongue, 2 pairs of lace holes. Sock stamped: 'Hush Puppies', style Saracen. c.1963. (d) One of a pair of exercise clogs with adjustable beige leather strap. Footshape toe, 1.4-inch heel. Rubber sole. Wooden base upcurved under metatarsal arch. Stamped on side: 'Dr Scholl's'. Made in West Germany. Size 6. Type worn outdoors and as indoor slippers, though designed only for short-term wear. Summer 1969.*

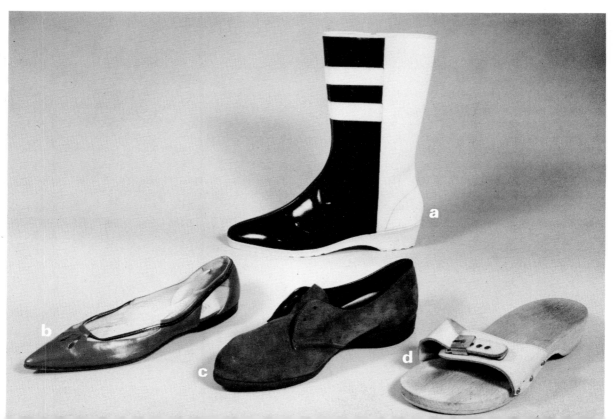

boot in 1979 with the pretty dresses, though still with the hint of a cowboy fringe.

SANDALS

Sandals were worn throughout the period with toes, heels, platforms (fig. 74c) following the general trend. At the time of the thigh boots, there were flat-soled sandals with cross-gartering to the thigh. But a curious fashion linked with the back-to-nature craze was the exercise clog (fig. 73d) worn as sandal or slipper from 1969, becoming less fashionable after 1972.

Altogether, this constitutes a fascinating period, especially from 1960 onwards as Britain, realizing the empire was lost and with a new generation questioning the standards of the establishment, searched for a new identity and roots. In 1960 there were styles derived from Victorian button shoes, in 1961 it was Victorian and Edwardian boots, including elastic sides. By 1965 the young were buying the originals to wear, regardless of condition, and boutiques sprang up to oblige. In 1962 and 1967 intermittently since, there have been 40s sling-backs. In 1970 it was 40s wedges, in 1971 Granny boots (Edwardian high legs), in 1972 it was back to late 40s Teddy Boys and ankle straps for women. In 1973 copying almost caught up with itself, with the revival of the 50s stiletto.

But more worrying were the copies of women's late 30s high-cut shoes. It happened in 1968, the year of the Paris student riots, in 1975, and again in 1979-80, the time of the Russian invasion of Afghanistan. Let us hope the young continue to let off pressure by expressing themselves in outrageous garb, and remind ourselves that we ignore what they are trying to say at our peril.

---

74 Women's shoes, boot and sandal. (a) One of a pair of black and yellow patent brogued lace shoes. Square toe, black cap, 1½-inch covered heel. Closed tab, black top, front lace, 5 pairs of eyelets, yellow lace. Size 7. Sock stamped: 'Varese Rotelli, Italy'. c.1965. (b) One of a pair of purple canvas boots. Rounded toe, 2½-inch covered straight heel, square at back. Rubber sole: 'Made in England'. Knee high, front lace over tongue, 13 pairs of hooks, black lace. Bought from Dolcis for £7, September 1970. (c) One of a pair of fawn hessian platform-sole sling-back sandals. Round toe, 2-inch covered platform rising to 4¾-inch brown covered wedge heel. Plastic sole. Sock stamped: 'Manfield. Made in France', summer 1975. (d) Blue suede court. Round peep toe, 4½-inch covered pyramid heel. Wrap-over front with cut-outs. Made by Newbold & Burton for Saxone Young Colony, autumn 1979.

Museums to Visit

Northampton Central Museum has the largest collection of footwear in Britain.
Clarks of Street Shoe Museum
Costume Museums:
  Museum of Costume, Bath
  Gallery of English Costume, Manchester
  Castle Howard Costume Gallery
There are very fine collections of shoes in:
  The Victoria and Albert Museum, London
  The Museum of London
  The Royal Scottish Museum, Edinburgh
In other shoe cities:
  The Newarke Houses Museum, Leicester
  The Bridewell Museum, Norwich

Most museums have a few shoes, though they may be in store. It is always worth enquiring at your local museum.

Further afield:
  Musée de la Chaussure, Romans-sur-Isère, France
  Deutsches Leder- und Schuhmuseum, Offenbach-am-Main, West Germany
  Nederlands Museum van Schoenen- Leder en Lederwaren, Waalwijk, Netherlands
  Bally Schuhmuseum, Schönenwerd, Switzerland
  Museo della Calzatura, Vigevano, Italy
  Museo del Calzado Antiguo, Barcelona, Spain
  Bata Shoe Museum, Toronto, Canada

Further Reading

Adams, H. *Footwear*. Oxford, Blackwell's Learning Library, 1976

Baynes, Ken & Kate, edited by. *The Shoe Show, British Shoes since 1790*. The Crafts Council, 1979.

Bordoli, E. *The Boot & Shoe Maker*. Gresham, 1935

Born, W. *The Development of Footwear*. CIBA Review, no.34. Basle, 1940

Brooke, Iris. *Footwear*. Pitman, 1972

Buck, Anne. *Dress in Eighteenth Century England*. Batsford, 1979
Victorian Costume and Costume Accessories. Herbert Jenkins, 1961

Clark, Roger & William. *Clark's of Street, 1829-1950*. 1950

Cremers-van der Does, E. Canter. *Van Schoenen en Schoenmakers*. Noorduijn, 1960

Crockett, H.G. et al. *The Modern Boot and Shoe Maker*. Gresham, 1917

Cunnington, C.W. & P. *Handbook of English Costume in the 17th Century*. Faber, 1973
Handbook of English Costume in the 18th century. Faber, 1972
Handbook of English Costume in the 19th century. Faber, 1970

Cunnington, C.W. *English Women's Clothing in the 19th century*. Faber, 1938
English Women's Clothing in the Present Century. Faber, 1952

Devlin, James. *The Guide to Trade, The Shoemaker*. Charles Knight, 1839

Dowie, James. *The Foot and its Covering*. Hardwicke, 1861

Ferragamo, Salvatore. *Shoemaker of Dreams*.

Harrap, 1957

Forrer, R. *Archäologisches zur Geschichte des Schuhes aller Zeiten*. Bally Schuhmuseum, 1942

Gall, P. Günter. *Deutsches Leder- und Schuhmuseum*, Katalog, Heft 6. 1980

Gillispie, edited by. *Diderot's Encyclopaedia of Trades and Industry*. Dover, 1959

Greig, T. Watson. *Ladies Old-fashioned Shoes*. Douglas, 1885

Hall, J. Sparkes. *The Book of the Feet*. Simpkin Marshall, 1848

Jaefvert, E. *Skomod och Skotillverkning fran Medeltiden till Vara Dagar*. Nordiska Museets, Stockholm, 1938

Lacroix, Paul. *Histoire de la Chaussure*. Delahays, Paris, 1862

Leno, J.B. *The Art of Boot and Shoe Making*. Crosby Lockwood, 1895

Lucas, A.T. *Footwear in Ireland*. County Louth Archaeological Journal XIII, 1956

Mansfield, Alan & Cunnington, P. *Handbook of English Costume in the 20th Century*. Faber, 1973

Quimby, Harold R. *Pacemakers of Progress*. Hide & Leather Publishing Co., Chicago, 1946

Redfern, W.B. *Royal and Historic Gloves and Shoes*. Methuen, 1904

Rees, John F. *The Art and Mystery of a Cordwainer*. London, 1813

Rossi, William A. *The Sex Life of the Foot and the Shoe*. Routledge & Kegan Paul, 1977

Roux, J.P. *La Chaussure*. Hachette, 1980

Sulser, Wilhelm. *Bally Austellung*. Felsgarten, Schönenwerd, 1948
A Brief History of the Shoe. Bally Schuhmuseum, 1958

Swann, J.M. *A History of Shoe Fashions*. Northampton Museum, 1975
Shoes Concealed in Buildings. Northampton Museum Journal 6, 1969
Catalogue of Shoe Buckles. Northampton Museum, 1981

Swaysland, E.J.C. *Boot and Shoe Design and Manufacture*. Tebbutt, 1905

Thornton, J.H., edited by. *Textbook of Footwear Manufacture*. Butterworth, 1970
Textbook of Footwear Materials. National Trade Press, 1955

Weber, Paul. *L'Histoire de la Chaussure*. A.T. Verlag, 1980

Weber, R.E.J. *'Postillionsstiefel'*. In *Waffen und Kostümkunde*, 1964, heft 1

Weldon, F.W. *A Norvic Century*. Jarrold, 1946

Wilcox, R. Turner. *The Mode in Footwear*. Charles Scribners, 1948

Wilson, Eunice. *A History of Shoe Fashion*. Pitman, 1969

Wright, Thomas. *The Romance of the Shoe*. Farncombe, 1922

For a more detailed list, including pre-1600, see *Shoe & Leather Bibliography*, Northampton Museum, 1976.

Glossary

with acknowledgement to J.H. Thornton:
A Glossary of Shoe Terms, Northampton, 1976.

Albert slipper with vamp extended upwards to form a tongue resting on the instep.

Apron front boot or shoe with oval-ended apron on top front, derived from the moccasin.

Back strap a strip of leather covering the back seam.

Balmoral a closed front ankle boot with golosh. Derby-bal or Eton-bal has the same golosh with open tab.

Bar shoe shoe with strap to button or buckle over instep; hence one-bar, two-bar etc.

Bellows tongue pleated tongue stitched in each side under lace holes.

Blucher open tab front lace boot, with straight side seam. Originally, quarters in one piece, with no back seam.

Bottom the underpart of shoes: soles, welt, heel.

Heel breast the front surface of a heel.

Brogue a lace shoe with many sections, each punched and serrated round the edge. Full brogues have winged cap.

Toe cap or tip extra reinforcement over the toe.

Clump a half-sole added to a shoe.

Counter an outside reinforcement on quarters.

Cuban heel a fairly straight-sided heel.

Derby a boot or shoe with the eyelet tabs stitched on top of the vamp, an open tab. Blucher, Gibson and Lorne are similar.

Domed toe end of the toe cut square at sole, with a shallow curved upper over it, blocked to shape, with puff inside.

Domed sole the sole is rounded up at the sides.

Finish colouring etc. on sole, to seal leather, channels etc.

Flesh the inner surface of a piece of leather originally next to the animal's body.

Forepart the front of the shoe, sole etc.

Ghillie a shoe of Scottish origin lacing through loops instead of eyelets.

Gibson See Derby.

Grain the outer surface of a piece of leather, originally bearing the hair etc. Uppers normally have the grain side outwards, except for suedes.

Grip kid or suede inside back of quarters, to prevent the shoe from slipping.

Golosh (1) an overshoe. (2) an extension of the vamp wings seamed at the back. *See* Balmoral.

Heel a component added to the rear end of the sole: either a block, usually covered, or separate lifts to form a stacked heel. The piece which rests on the ground is called the top piece.

Insole the inside bottom part of a shoe on which the foot rests.

Instep the area on top of the foot.

Lasting shaping the upper to the last.

Latchet the top fronts of the quarters extended into straps.

Lift See Heel.

Louis heel a heel of which the breast is covered with a downward extension of the sole.

Monk shoe shoe with quarters extending over tongue, usually fastened with strap and buckle.

Moccasin a foot bag — the sole curving up to seam over the foot.

Mule shoe without heel quarters.

Oxford closed tab lace shoe, the eyelet tabs being stitched under the vamp.

Pass line the widest point at the ankle of a boot.

Peg strip of wood at first oval in section for securing heel lifts; in the nineteenth century diamond section, for soles.

Quarters the sides of a shoe upper joining the vamp at the front, and each other at the back of the heel. If seamed here, it is called the back seam.

Rand a narrow strip of leather in the sole or heel seams.

Rivet a metal nail knocked through the sole against an iron or iron-plated last, to turn the tip over and prevent it coming out.

Sandal a sole, with straps to hold it on the foot.

Shank a reinforcement in the waist of a shoe, between sole and insole, necessary when the shoe has a heel.

Sling-back a shoe with a strap round the back of the ankle in place of quarters.

Sock material inside the shoe covering all or part of the insole.

Spanish heel a high thin heel with curved breast, like the louis.

Stiffener a reinforcement inside the quarters.

Stiletto heel a thin heel with tiny top piece.

Straights shoes made symmetrical, for either foot, not right and left.

Sole stamp stamp to seal holes made by nails used to attach sole to last before attaching to upper.

Throat the centre of the rear end of the vamp resting on the instep of the foot.

Toe puff a reinforcement inside the toe end of the vamp.

Toe spring the elevation of the toe end of a shoe above the horizontal surface on which the shoe stands.

Tongue an extension of the vamp under the latchets.

Top edge the top of uppers.

Top piece the bottom piece of the heel which rests on the ground.

Tunnel stitch the hole enters the surface of the leather, passes a short distance between grain and flesh, to reappear on the same side.

Turnshoe shoe made inside out and then turned, leaving sole seam on the inside.

Upper the part which covers the top of the foot. It normally consists of vamp, quarters and lining.

Vamp the front section of a shoe upper, covering the toes and part of the instep.

Veldtschoen a shoe in which the upper is turned outwards along the bottom edge, to which the sole is attached.

Waist the narrow part under the arch of the foot and sole.

Walled toe a toe which rises vertically from the sole and turns sharply across the top of the foot.

Wedge heel a heel extending under the waist of the shoe to the forepart.

Welt a narrow strip of leather sewn round the edge of the upper and insole. The sole is then attached to the welt.

Wheeling an iron is sometimes wheeled over the sole and seat seams to seal them, either ridged, or more fancy patterns, such as crow.

See Martin W. Wright: *The Shoeman's Foreign Terms*, Halford, 1921, pp.72-107, 'Technical Dictionary and Types of British Footwear,' with illustrations. Some pages are reproduced here, with the key.

TYPES OF BRITISH FOOTWEAR – KEY

The names are generally correct for either ladies' or
gents' patterns, and where this is so, illustration of
only one or the other is given.

A Golosh
   a. Joined
   b. Brogued
   c. Circular
B Vamp
C Apron
D Leg
E Quarter
F Counter
G Front
H Back
   a. Whole
   b. Joined
I Toe-cap
   a. Straight
   b. Peak
   c. Half Peak
   d. Wing
J Button piece
   a. Straight
   b. Wave
   c. Scallop
   d. Reverse
K Facing
   a. Stitching
   b. Inside
   c. Outside
L Backstrap
   a. Jockey backstrap
   b. Backstrap loop
M Loop

N Topband
O Lining
P Collar
Q Insertion
R Gusset
S Tongue
T Tab
U Bar
V Binding
W Hooks
X Eyelets
Y Slide
Z Bow
2 Pom pom
3 Crimped
4 Broguing
5 Heel
   a. Cuban
   b. Curved Cuban
   c. Semi Cuban
   d. Military
   e. Louis
   f. Semi louis
   g Louis Cuban
   h. German seat, or out-
         standing heel
6 Heel breast
7 Heel tip
8 Top piece
9 Clump
10 Waist

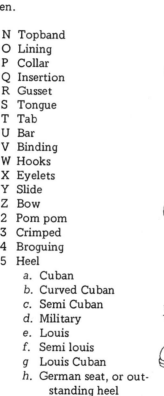

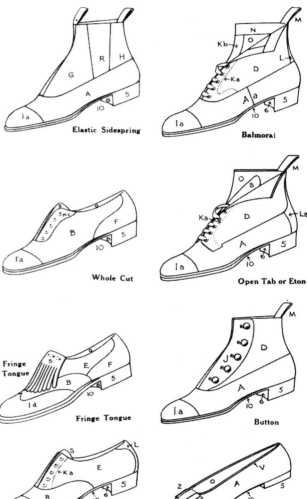

Elastic Sidespring

Balmoral

Whole Cut

Open Tab or Eton

Fringe Tongue

Button

Oxford

Court

Derby

Ascot Derby

Chelsea

Columbia Buckle Boot

Norwegian

Blucher

Gibson or Derby Shoe

Brogue

Dominion

Greek Court

Dual Bar

Cross Bar

Bandeau

Grecian

Turkish

Plimsoll

Albert

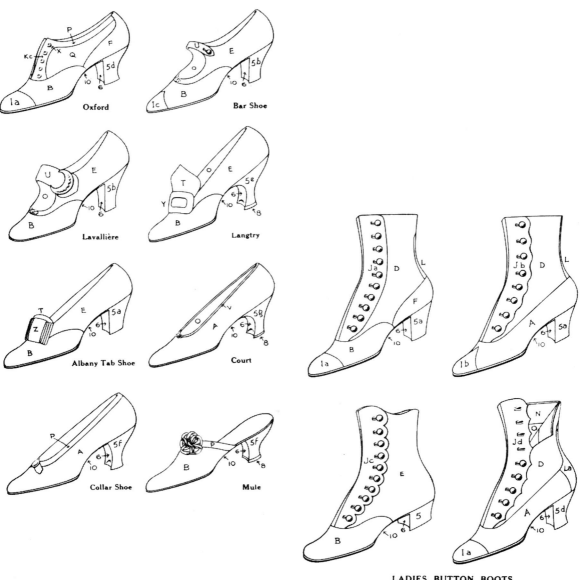

Oxford

Bar Shoe

Lavallière

Langtry

Albany Tab Shoe

Court

Collar Shoe

Mule

LADIES BUTTON BOOTS
Shewing four distinct button pieces.

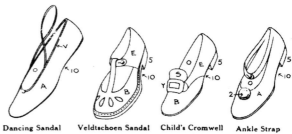

Dancing Sandal Veldtschoen Sandal Child's Cromwell Ankle Strap

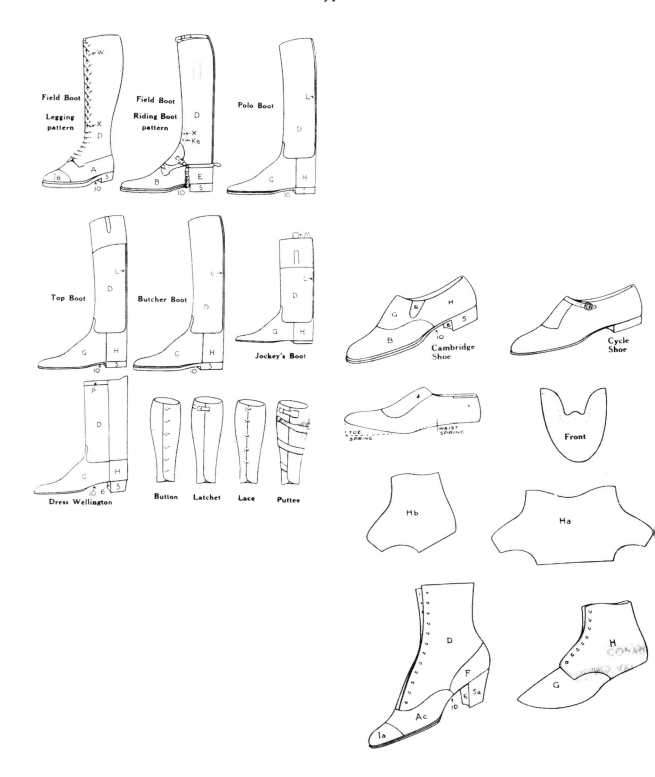

Field Boot

Legging
pattern

Field Boot

Riding Boot
pattern

Polo Boot

Top Boot

Butcher Boot

Jockey's Boot

Dress Wellington

Button   Latchet   Lace   Puttee

Cambridge
Shoe

Cycle
Shoe

TOE SPRING   WAIST SPRING

Front

Index

95

DATE			